CW01669432

:(Less Perfect More Happy :)

CHRIS WARD

:(Less Perfect *More Happy* :)
www.friendfulness.com
password: friendful

FOR EXTRA BONUS CONTENT

Plus a community of less perfect, more happy people, keen to share friendship, stories and time together.

Facebook: Friendfulness – Less Perfect *More Happy*

Credits

The book contains a number of extracts from other books and media articles. They are included by kind permission of the author or their publishers. All the experts have direct experience of perfectionism, report on it or work in the field of positive mental health, and so I recommend further reading of their work if you wish to understand more.

I would like to thank the following (and their publishers) for the contribution their writing has made to the understanding of perfectionism.

Sir Al Aynsley-Green
Adrian Bethune
Alain de Botton
Brené Brown
Jake Chapman
Thomas Curran of the University of Bath
Matt Dickinson
Beverly Engel
Sir Alex Ferguson
Rebecca Greenfield
Richard Godwin
Amie Henderson
Andrew P. Hill of York St John University
Jean Liedloff
Anne Longfield
Dr Gabor Mate
Davina McCall
Sir Michael Moritz
Ann Mroz
Dr Gordon Neufeld
Marisa Peer
Victoria Pendleton CBE
Amanda Ruggeri
Cordelia Sigurdsson
Fiona Sturges
Ruth Whippman
Bradley Wiggins
Brian Wilson

Full publishing details and links to their work can be found at www.friendfulness.com

Advance praise for
:(Less Perfect *More Happy* :)

'A crucial insight into a misunderstood disorder and a tonic for anyone struggling with the unattainable urge to be perfect.'

Dave Cornthwaite, the Yes man, world record-breaking author and filmmaker

'My heart breaks when I see young people struggling with the constant perception of having to be "perfect", just so that they feel they fit in. This book opens the door to their very private world and enables us to understand them and the secret battles that they endure.'

Andria Zafirakou, Global Teacher of the Year

'This is such an important story for our times, told with inspiring vulnerability. The insights from Chris's journey will stay with you long after you put the book down.'

Kim Hudson, US author and speaker

'I'd strongly encourage those of us who put our obsession with achieving in sport, ahead of everything else in their life, to read this book and learn how we can still achieve, but that people love us already. We don't need to cycle around the world to prove anything to anybody.'

Sean Conway, world-record-breaking adventurer

'Chris covers not only important aspects of obsessiveness but provides moving personal testimony to the painful costs of these and suggestions as to how to make healthy change.'

Allan E. Mallinger and Jeannette De Wyze, authors of *Too Perfect*

'Readers will be able to associate with a lot, not realising perfectionism is the cause. It comforts, inspires, challenges and encourages in equal measure. I want every member of my family to read it, to understand our conflicts.'

Clare Hester, business leader

Acknowledgements

I am not a writer and this book is certainly not perfect. However, what perfectionism *really* is, what causes it, what lengths it leads sufferers to go to – and especially how they can overcome it – need to be fully understood. I want to thank the following people who have helped to do that:

Len Aaron
Fiona Andreanelli
Jeremy Ashworth
Hilary Brown
Constantinos Carastavrakis
JC Carroll
Frank Chambers
Ged Equi
Hugo Gerrard
Trevor Gray
Robert Hamilton
Clare Hester
Kim Hudson
Will King
Sue Lacey
Vicky Lambert
Tony Matthews
Jonny Miller
Daniel Ormondroyd
Alice Pack
Ravi Ruperal
Danny Russell
Alison Rust
Peigi Series
Tony Soutter
Joanne Tomlinson
Tim Tucker
Neil Nash Williams

For Helen, Molly, Bob, Rose and Audrey.

My parents, siblings, friends, colleagues and teammates.

This explains a lot.

Sorry.

Contents

Introduction I'm not good enough 1

Prologue Two sides to every story 7

Part One Childhood 15
Age 4 The best years… 17
Age 5 Looking up to your parents 19
Age 6 A disappointment 22
Age 7 Who do you want to be? 25
Age 8 Doing what you're told 29
Age 9 Just the way it is 32
Age 10 The best days…? 36
Age 11 Trying your best 41
Age 12 Behind the bedroom door 43
Age 13 Sorry 46
Age 14 Thatcher's children 48
Age 15 Can always do better 51
Age 16 Everyone's laughing at you 54
Age 17 There's no such word as can't 60
Age 18 Collaborate and Compromise 67
Age 19 Not good enough teenager 70

Part Two Chasing perfection 77
Age 20 Perfectionist adult 79
Age 21 Have to put it right 84
Age 22 Finding your tribe 87
Age 23 Trying to prove everyone wrong 90
Age 24 Nothing will prove everyone wrong 93
Age 25 Paying your way 96
Age 26 An obsession 99
Age 27 Perfectionist friend 101
Age 28 Perfectionist lover 106
Age 29 All about the timing 111

Part Three Success and family life 115
Age 30 Going Travelling 117
Age 31 Meeting the right person 120
Age 32 A good day at work 125
Age 33 Perfectionist parent 127
Age 34 Maintaining a stiff upper lip 130
Age 35 Perfectionist boss 134
Age 36 Behind every Successful perfectionist … 139
Age 37 Behind every rich perfectionist … 144
Age 38 Counselling 148
Age 39 Perfectionist employee 153

Part Four Repercussions 157
Age 40 Procrastinator 159
Age 41 Perfectionist sports player 161
Age 42 Back to nature 168
Age 43 Perfectionist holidaymaker 172
Age 44 (I) Perfectionist partner and parent 175
Age 44 (II) Perfectionist ex-partner and single parent 182
Age 45 Staying vigilant 185
Age 46 (I) Important truths remain unspoken 188
Age 46 (II) Important truths are heard 190
Age 47 Keep it simple 193
Age 48 Hard feelings 196
Age 49 Loved 200

Part Five Overcoming perfectionism 209
Age 50 (I) Access the inner circle 211
Age 50 (II) Clear communication 214
Age 51 Perfectionist world 218
Age 52 Overcoming perfectionism 222
Age 53 (I) Failing and learning 228
Age 53 (II) Less perfect, more scale 230
Age 54 Good enough partner 232
Age 55 Good enough parent 237
Age 56 Good enough life 241
Age 57 Good enough world 244

Attached booklets How to overcome perfectionism
How to enjoy a less perfect, more happy world

Published in 2019 by
Blue Dot World Ltd
105 Wendell Road
London W12 9SD

Contact the publisher for all requests
helen@bluedotworld.com
Friendfulness.com

Design and Typesetting by Fiona Andreanelli
Cover design by Ged Equi
Photography by Rose Ward
Printed in Great Britain by Empress Litho Limited

ISBN 978-0-9576123-7-2

All information was accurate at time of going to press.
Any inadvertent omissions can be rectified in future editions.

A CIP catalogue record for this book is available from the British Library.

The publisher supports the Forest Stewardship Council® (FSC®), the leading international forest certification organisation. This book is made from acid-free paper from an FSC®-certified provider. FSC is the only forest-certification scheme supported by the leading environmental organisations, including Greenpeace.

:(Introduction :)

If you are striving to do something as well as you possibly can, to do it *perfectly* even, because it is important to you or because you believe you will enjoy it or its potential rewards, that is a natural and a positive ambition. That's good.

That is not perfectionism though. Perfectionism isn't good. Perfectionists are the most misunderstood people in society, often even misunderstood by themselves.

We're all born with imperfections, individual traits that make us different. But for some of us, at some point during our childhood, we genuinely start to believe that compared to everyone else, some aspect of ourselves isn't good enough and it feels like everyone is judging us for our imperfections.

In later life, attempting to recover our feel-good factor, some people buy brands with promise for feeling cooler, younger, healthier. Some struggle with anxiety and depression, some turn to one more drink, drug or bet. Some even try to become famous, hoping that will provide the answer. We attempt anything that promises an escape from insecurity and a return to the warmth of acceptance for who we really are, not who we think people want us to be.

An increasing number now believe if they can convince themselves and everyone else they are good enough, if they make certain things they think, say and do absolutely perfect, if they can make aspects of their work, their body, their friendships and their family perfect, then they can finally 'achieve' the happiness they recall feeling as a small child.

So, what do they do? They dedicate their adult life to trying to prove themselves to all the people they share their lives with, all day and every day, at the expense of their actual relationships with them. They become perfectionists.

Perfectionism is so little understood that it often leads to perfectionists being completely misunderstood – especially by those with whom they battle on a daily basis as they struggle to achieve the elusive perfectionism and its mythical promise. The myth is that in achieving perfection the perfectionist will finally prove they can be flawless, that it is the only way they will ever get to once again experience the feeling they are 'good enough'.

But achieving 'perfection' can never make us happy, contented or feel unconditionally loved. Instead perfectionism lurks behind the epidemic of social and mental-health issues, relationship breakdowns, workaholism, anxiety, depression, burnout, loneliness and self-harm.

If society can understand what perfectionism really is and reduce its causes, we can reduce our mental health and social issues, reduce relationship breakdowns, obsessions, extreme politics, conflict, bullying, road rage, food issues, wasted time and wasted lives.

If we all understand perfectionism, individuals will lead happier lives and the world will be a far more harmonious place.

Definitions

Perfectionism and OCPD

Together with all its associated traits, perfectionism is classed as a personality disorder[1], known as obsessive compulsive personality disorder (OCPD), and has been identified as one of the most prevalent but most misunderstood disorders. The conclusion of the research paper 'Perfectionism is Increasing over Time: A Meta-Analysis of Birth Cohort Differences From 1989 to 2016' by T. Curran of the University of Bath and P. Hill of York St John University was that it has now reached epidemic proportions. This was echoed and reported on globally by many contemporary commentators: 'Perfectionism is destroying the mental health of the millennial generation' (*The Guardian*); 'Perfectionism is the misunderstood global epidemic that is affecting up to two in five of us' (BBC); 'The rise of perfectionism is negatively affecting young people' (World

1 OCPD is classed as a personality disorder under code F60.5 of the American ICD-10-CM (diagnosis) and ICD-10-PCS (procedure) medical coding references and DSM-5 301.4 in *The Diagnostic and Statistical Manual of the American Psychiatric Association.*

Economic Forum); 'The hidden epidemic of perfectionism' (CBS News); and 'Perfectionism is increasing and that is not good news' (*Harvard Business Review*).

OCPD is not OCD

OCPD and obsessive compulsive disorder (OCD) are quite different disorders, with only minimal crossover of sufferers or symptoms. Both do involve the tendency to obsess, act compulsively, hoard things, and often to keep things orderly and, to some degree, symmetrical. While OCD is an illness that can develop at any point, OCPD must have begun by early adulthood and refers to a deeply embedded personality disorder. Thus, while people with OCD do not want to have the troubling thoughts they have and realize that those thoughts are irrational and unreasonable, those with OCPD believe their thinking and behaviour are perfectly rational and normal. Confusion between the conditions is a major factor in the lack of awareness of the often severe consequences of perfectionism and OCPD to mental health.

'I'm not good enough!'

The feeling of not being 'good enough' dictated almost my entire life. It dictated what I thought, the decisions I made, and the actions I took. This largely meant avoiding other people and not prioritizing doing anything that might be considered enjoyable, until I had proven that I was good enough. I was on a mission – a mission impossible, as I was later to learn.

I couldn't be myself with other people. I didn't really have any real friends. I never switched off from work. I never relaxed. I felt lonely. I *was* lonely.

But it's only now I know that I wasn't alone.

After a lifetime of being a perfectionist, three years of research and long conversations with fellow sufferers and experts I now understand what perfectionism is, where it can stem from, the damage it caused to my mental health and every one of my relationships, and, most thankfully, how to manage it. Not to overcome it completely, though: once a perfectionist always a perfectionist, as I found while trying to finish writing this book.

My story isn't special or different. It just normally remains hidden and stays untold and I couldn't have written this book when I was suffering badly. Like most people, I didn't even know perfectionism was anything other than just trying to do my best. And what's wrong with that? All I knew was that I argued with my wife, that I always tried my best at everything to prove to my dad I was good enough, and that I was a workaholic. But I just thought that was 'normal' or 'natural'. It was normal to need everything done my way, despite the silences, arguments and resentment that seemed to follow me around.

Now, though, I am in a contented place, a place where I can relax, yes, but where far more importantly, those around me can also relax. I've stopped judging them and everything they do by perfectionism's obsessively high standards.

But the journey to get here has taken me, my family and closest friends through the very worst places. When I had achieved far more than I thought possible and still didn't feel 'good enough', what did I do? I blamed and fought with the people who meant the most to me.

In my late thirties perfectionism led to me separating from my wife, Helen, and leaving the family home we shared with our children ... So, it's there where this story, for the moment, begins.

How this book works

The book is laid out as a series of chronological incidents in the author's life, each exploring what perfectionism really is and how it effects sufferers' lives. Each chapter is interspersed with book extracts and media articles that feature well-known people or incidents of a similar nature, and concludes with a collated exposition of the views of mental-health experts.

:(Prologue :)

Two sides to every story

The public face ...

I had just had some success at work and it led to *PR Week* publishing an article about my career. I've included the text here, not to show off, but to give an insight into how wrongly a perfectionist's life can be perceived from the outside: to the outsider I was at the pinnacle of my career and was living the perfect life. To the insiders, my wife and children, my friends, myself, it was a very different scenario.

PROFILE: CHRIS WARD, BEATWAX COMMUNICATIONS

Ward... *'People do not leave Beatwax. I do not wear a suit. We have a culture and that is still there.'*

A cocktail of energy, drive and creativity

After Friends Reunited, Beatwax CEO Chris Ward is keen for new challenges

Chris Ward's main claim to fame in his seven years of managing bands was handling the support act that toured with Debbie Harry. But as a PR impresario he has made an indelible mark as the man who delivered the coverage for web phenomenon Friends Reunited.

This work shot Ward's agency, Beatwax Communications, to the fore. Along ...

... brand had critical mass in terms of member numbers when journalists came on board.

Having pocketed an undisclosed sum from the sale of Beatwax, Ward has seen the agency double in size to 45 staff in 18 months, with a turnover of £4.5m-a-year. Ongoing work includes replacing Stella Artois's seven-year-old outdoor screening ... with a new push featuring 'chill-out ...

DIARY

Freud has no ...

An astonishing coi...
report this week. Jus...
we confirm in prin...
that Freud Commu...
to bag roughly £500...
from internet giant...
year, Matthew Freu...
featured puffing his...
in the 'aficionado' ...
GQ magazine.

Avid *GQ* reader...
the format – the subj...
to name which pr...
uses in certain cate...
CDs, hotels, the web ...

Freud's response...
even hardened cy...
'Service providers ...
been over-promisi...
der-delivering. Unt...
is. AOL Broadban...
is a quantum leap i...
internet multimed...
It's the realisation – ...

Green... *knows his* ...

Green leads th... Unilever reigns ...

FMCG giant Unil...
up at last week's *I*...
annual awards at...
Grosvenor House ...
event, hosted by Ro...
was a triumph for ...
relations team, ...
seven awards, most ...
Grand Prix for B...
Investor Relation...
included Most Pro...
and Best Disclosure ...

Headline from *PR Week* – my real life couldn't have been more different

Chris Ward's main claim to fame in his seven years of managing bands was handling the support act that toured with Debbie Harry. But as a PR impresario he has made an indelible mark as the man who delivered the coverage for web phenomenon Friends Reunited.

This work shot Ward's agency to the fore. Along with a track record in music, film and campaigns for brands such as Stella Artois, the Friends Reunited work prompted last year's lucrative sale of his agency.

Ward is an energetic cocktail of entrepreneur, good Samaritan and hard-drinking football supporter.

Ward's rise can be tracked through his ability to spot a gap in the market. He kicked off his career, aged 23, managing obscure bands but in 1992 saw an opportunity when the Tories said they would dramatically boost student numbers. Ward went through complex negotiations with student unions to target students for brands and formed Beatwax to run this.

This background may have helped him win work with Friends Reunited joint founder Steve Pankhurst. Pankhurst recalls their first meeting, 'We went to his office and it was a complete tip. He was late, nobody knew what they were doing and there were crates of Stella Artois lying around'. Unlike the other agencies Pankhurst saw, whose staff wore suits and ties and 'gave us the corporate line', Ward spoke the 'same language'. He adds 'Chris was on the same wavelength as us.'

Having pocketed an undisclosed sum for the sale of Beatwax, Ward has seen the agency double in size to 45 staff in 18 months, with a turnover of £4.5 million a year.

Ward says his next major challenge is to boost member numbers at another of his innovations, Hollywood research firm Firstmovies.

With that and Beatwax, a young family and a new nostalgia card business to run with his wife, Ward has his work cut out..

Simon Ellery, *PR Week*

... The private story
Later the same day with a marriage guidance counsellor

'Helen?' prompted the counsellor. 'What do you think?'

'Where do you want me to start? We are really struggling. Chris doesn't ever relax and never seems to be content with what we have. And we do have everything we need.

'He's a frustrated and frustrating workaholic. When he comes through the door, the children don't know if he's going to be happy Dad or annoyed with them. Is he going to play with them or is he going to be picky about something that doesn't really matter? The same goes for me really.

'I'm wondering: will he moan that the dinner isn't ready yet? Will he think the kids' bedrooms are untidy or complain that I haven't got four quotes for some work we need doing? We walk on eggshells around him.

'He can't seem to stop himself saying exactly what he thinks, and sometimes that hurts. The truth can hurt but he doesn't see that.

'How is the relationship between the two of you?' the counsellor probed.

'He doesn't get it when I'm joking. He can go quiet, which must be because I have said something wrong. He disappears to his little office or on his bike. It's when he seems most contented, when he's away from us, when he's in his own world. It's like we're an annoyance. His family is a hindrance to him.

'He makes us feel like we always have to do what he suggests. He won't ever discuss it; we're not allowed to say no. Although to be fair, we normally have a good time when we do go out. He has good ideas!'

I smile, but only inside.

My wife continues. 'At work, he's the boss and everyone has to agree with him. But if I don't, he says I'm the only person who doesn't think he's any good. Too many of our conversations end in an argument and I feel useless. It's impossible being married to someone who always thinks they're right.

'When I need some emotional support, a cuddle perhaps, he just gives me advice. I don't want any more bloody advice.'

I smile, a sort of grimace this time, a very faint, very knowing smile. My wife and the counsellor didn't see it, though. Again, it was only inside my head.

'It feels like we hardly ever see the real him, just this driven, determined force of nature. He's achieved so much; we've done so many amazing things. We seem to be on a journey doing loads of crazy things until he finds contentment. He won't stop until he's happy and he's never happy.

'At our worst, we have had some very bad, very loud arguments in the kitchen, pretty much in front of the kids, if they hadn't sloped off to their bedrooms to escape it, to escape us, their parents. It normally descends to its worst point when we are just arguing about the argument! About who said what, or what they did or did not mean. We go into ridiculous, minute detail and forget what we were arguing about in the first place. It's driving me mad. Literally!

'Driving me mad. Can you hear me? Can you hear me, Chris?! We are hurting the children. I hate what it must be doing to them, what "we" are doing to them.

'It is difficult to love him. But I do love him. We all love him. Our friends love him. But I just can't go on like this. The kids don't deserve this.

'I just want us to be happy together, a happy family, for Chris to be happy with us and happy with himself.'

'Chris?' the counsellor said, turning to me for some comment, to hear *my* side perhaps.

I couldn't speak.

In case I cried.

'Chris?'

I swallowed hard.

It was true.

It was *all* true.

Obviously, I couldn't actually say that out loud.

I hated it. I hated it. I hated it. This was everything I didn't want. Everything I'd spent my whole life trying not to be. I'm just a kid from a little bedroom in suburbia. I can't believe anyone would ever love me, that I have wonderful children and all I'm doing is ruining everyone's life.

I didn't want to argue with Helen. I desperately wanted us to just be normal but I hated my job; it wasn't real. I couldn't be myself there, and I was taking it out on them.

I'd tried my whole life not to be my dad but to impress him. And now I was just my dad: always at work and when I did come home, just telling my children off for no real reason. I couldn't help myself. I hate it. I hate it.

I hate me.

I still didn't say anything.

'Chris, what about you?' the counsellor persisted.

'Where do you want me to start?'

'At the beginning …'

:(Part One :)
Childhood

AGE 4
The best years …

My happiest childhood memories are of playing with my friends in the orchard at playschool. It felt like we were on an adventure and I loved it – although I was always scared of the spiders. I just loved being with my friends: playing football, riding our bikes and just hanging out, talking, telling funny jokes, doing nothing in particular.

But I also loved it when I went home.

I lived with Mum and Dad and my two sisters, Sue and Sandra. I was the oldest. I had the smallest bedroom to myself; my sisters shared the biggest. We had three apple trees in the back garden, one for each of us kids. Every summer Dad would hold a competition to see whose tree grew the most apples.

Dad designed things for his job. I didn't know what exactly, but he once put a plastic thing on my head and said he was testing it for oxygen levels. I did know, though, that he rode a bicycle and wore horrible cycling gear.

My mum was a typist. She won competitions by typing over a hundred words a minute. I also thought she had invented cheesecake. I had never seen it anywhere else, except on our kitchen worktop, on Sunday afternoons, when I'd run my finger around the edge of it when she wasn't looking. I lived under that illusion until our first ever visit to the theatre. It was during the interval, when she bought a slice for me and explained that no, she hadn't invented it. I was really disappointed.

I loved these early years of childhood: climbing the bus stairs as quickly as possible to get the front seats, on our way to Grandma's and a slice of her homemade cake; building camps in the woods after school, sandcastles in the summer and snowmen in the winter. I love these memories.

I had a very normal childhood. I listened to tens of thousands of songs, scored the odd goal in football, watched hundreds of episodes of my favourite TV programmes, attended hundreds of days of school, played nonstop in the field across the road, rode lots of miles on my bike, ran dozens of wet, slow miles of school cross-country, collected hundreds of football stickers, played lots of games and listened to thousands of hours of radio.

I did hundreds of things, my parents said thousands of things to me, and I saw millions of things in the world around me.

I was happy and contented. I had the best friends and the best family.

I didn't want anything to ever change. I didn't want to grow up.

Life was perfect back then.

My sister and I in the local newspaper

AGE 5
Looking up to your parents

Mum was always at home when we got back from school because she seemed to live in the kitchen. But we didn't see nearly as much of Dad. He was always somewhere else – at work, in the shed or riding his bike. I would see him briefly at breakfast, teatime and occasionally – though only if we'd been good – at bedtime when he'd read us a story.

We loved it when he did. He was great at making up stories, rather than just reading one out of a book. He would make them scarier and more fun, and I would get to be the hero. When I'd been good and he would read a story to us, they were the best times I ever spent with my dad.

Like most fathers in our street, Dad was normally busy doing literally anything and everything:

- mending the car or a bicycle
- making furniture for the home
- knowing all the answers to my homework
- knowing right from wrong
- mending any broken toys
- making a desk for my bedroom
- cycling hundreds of miles.

He did a lot for me, for which I showed him nothing but complete respect. I didn't feel close to him, though. I was in awe of him.

He was very tall and thin, too bristly and not very cuddly. He was what was called a 'real man'. He never wasted time watching TV or listening to music with us. He would rather be working, making something useful, or out cycling. He was always cycling. I really can't remember him just lying on the sofa, doing nothing, with the rest of us. Maybe because he never did. It meant that we felt a bit guilty every time we did just sit and watch TV.

If we made too much noise or went to try to get him to play with us, Mum would usually tell us to 'stop annoying your father'.

Dad taught me, very sternly, that smoking and drugs were bad for me. I never touched either as a child. I've never touched them as an adult either. I didn't see the things he did for me as signs of love, more as his fatherly duties. I just wanted to be good for him so he would tell me a story, tickle me and then give me a cuddle.

I felt inferior and a bit scared of him, but that felt right. I thought that was how you should feel about your father. If anyone ever threatened me, I was confident enough to respond, 'I'll tell my dad.' And it seemed to make anyone I thought was going to do something horrible to me stop in their tracks.

Cause: perfect parents

Perfectionism is more prevalent in eldest children, whose role models have been the overcautious 'perfect' parents of their first child, rather than the 'imperfect' older sibling and, by then, the much less cautious parents of an expanding family.

Workaholic parents justify their workaholism by telling themselves that they are sacrificing time with their children to build their career and income 'for the good of the family'. But almost any child will tell you they would prefer their parents to spend more time with them than spend more money on them.

Not having enough time with their parents can lead to children feeling inadequate and not worthy of their attention. This simple, and rectifiable, cause leaves many children with the lifelong feeling that they have to achieve something significant in order to attract the loving attention of their parents – attention that they innately feel they should receive unconditionally when young.

Victoria Pendleton CBE is one of Britain's most successful female Olympians. As a cyclist she was gold medallist at European, World and Olympic level and winner of nine world titles. Since the end of her professional cycling career she has competed at the highest level in horse racing, taken part in endurance challenges and attempted to climb Mount Everest. Victoria's father was her perfect role model and she has described herself as 'a self-critical perfectionist.' Below is an extract from the first page of her autobiography '*Between the lines*'.

Dad rode away from me as we climbed the hill on a cold and drizzly Sunday morning in Bedfordshire. 'He doesn't love me,' I said to myself as I tried to keep up with the distant figure of my father. 'He doesn't love me. He doesn't love me ...'

I repeated the words over and over again as, never lifting my gaze from the unbreakable man on the bike climb on the steep hill, I turned my legs as fast as I could. I had to hang on to Dad. I was sure if I lost sight of him I would lose hold of his love.

The drizzle hardened into rain. Dad still didn't look back. He sped away from me, up towards the clouds rolling down from the top of the hill. Dad looked more ghostly then.

I had grown used to the ritual of chasing my father as he sped ahead of me. Dad dealt in clear and simple truths. He never told you that you were better than you were – even to boost you at your most vulnerable. Dad just expected you to do your best every single day. He was tough but, when I pleased him, I felt radiant with happiness. I knew how much it meant when Dad said he was proud of me.

Days and climbs such as these, Dad said, were 'character building'. That old-fashioned phrase covered everything that was mean and testing because what didn't kill you made you stronger. But I didn't care about building my character.

I just wanted Dad to slow down and show me that he loved me.

AGE 6
A disappointment

I would have been home from school for a few hours, watched some TV in the lounge with my sisters, had a biscuit and we'd probably be in our bedrooms playing, before we would hear the back door go … and be slightly wary.

It would be Dad, home from work.

Ninety-nine times out of a hundred he'd chat to Mum and then we'd all have tea together. None of us was allowed to get down from the kitchen table and go back up to our rooms until we'd eaten everything on our plate and said grace – unless, that was we mucked about, in which case we'd be back in our bedrooms 'before our feet could touch the ground'.

Unfortunately, I mainly remember the few times when Dad came in and would call us downstairs to the kitchen and just question us. And if he wasn't happy with the answers, he'd tell us off, for what felt like no reason other than he was in a bad mood.

"Why haven't you helped your mother lay the table? Whose mess is that in the lounge? Have you cleaned your bedrooms? Finished your homework? How can you do your homework with that music playing? Come on, do what I say … *Now*!"

It could be about anything, we never knew what was coming next.

Very occasionally we did know what was coming, because Mum had told us off earlier and brought a pause to proceedings by saying, 'Wait till your father comes home and I tell him what you've done.' The periods between her informing us of that and the sound of the door opening were never the best of times.

Cause: parental (mis)communication

Psychologists agree that there is rarely one single thing that causes OCPD/perfectionism to develop but that it most likely arises out of a series of experiences in which the child perceives themselves or the things around them as 'not right'.

Parents should be aware that, whether deliberately or through misunderstanding, they can make their children feel as though they are a disappointment to them, making them feel less loved as a consequence, often due to their stressed reaction to simple childish behaviour they don't approve of.

Communication between adults and children often leads to this type of misunderstanding. Young children can easily translate a parent's pride as love for them or frustration as disappointment in them. Parents can struggle with returning daily to their messy home and unruly children, a situation they can't control, without resorting to an unfair, probably unreasonable, punishment to try to retain some control.

If adults reacted like this with other adults, there would be confrontation, but they do it knowing their children are the ones that won't answer them back. They are too young and respectful to do anything other than be obedient and do what they are told. They are the ones they can control. The ones they unfortunately start to distance themselves from.

We can help reduce the opportunity for perfectionism to develop in children by thinking carefully about how we discipline and communicate with them. To make sure there is no misunderstanding between how much we feel for them and how we communicate our expectations, rules and discipline.

Try to take a moment before you step through the front door and decide if it is worth ruining your child's unfettered feelings, by arguing or punishing them. It almost hardly ever is.

Beverly Engel is an internationally recognized psychotherapist and acclaimed advocate for victims of emotional abuse. The following extract is taken from her book *The Nice Girl Syndrome.*

There are many ways that parents make their children feel they are a disappointment to them, including ...

BELITTLING. 'You're too old to want to be held' or 'You're just a cry-baby' are horribly humiliating to a child or when a parent makes a negative comparison between their child and another, such as 'Why can't you act like them? See how they sit quietly while their mother is talking' it is not only humiliating but teaches a child to always compare himself or herself with peers and find himself deficient by comparison.

BLAMING. Many parents blame and berate the child if they make a mistake, like breaking something 'You stupid idiot! Do you think money grows on trees? I don't have money to buy another one!' This shames the child to such an extent that he or she cannot find a way to walk away from the situation with his or her head held high.

CONTEMPT. Expressions of disgust or contempt communicate absolute rejection. The look of contempt, often a sneer or a raised upper lip, especially from someone who is significant to a child, can make them feel disgusting or offensive.

HUMILIATION. As Gershen Kaufman stated in his book Shame: The Power of Caring, 'There is no more humiliating experience than to have an adult who is clearly the stronger and more powerful take advantage of that power and give us a beating.' (verbal or physical).

DISABLING EXPECTATIONS. When a child becomes aware of the real possibility of failing to meet parental expectations, he or she often experiences a binding self-consciousness. This painful watching of oneself is disabling. When something is expected of us in this way attaining a goal is made harder, if not impossible.

AGE 7
Who do you want to be?

My hero was Bobby Moore, the captain of the England football team and the only English player to ever lift the World Cup. He was certainly the most famous English footballer; many said he was the best in the world … Now he was coming to the local petrol garage to sign autographs. And Dad was taking me to see him!

We had to queue up for ages, but I've never seen a happier queue. This was the England football captain, in a petrol station, in my home town.

When we finally got to the front, he signed a postcard, gave me a special World Cup football coin and asked what my name was. I was too shy to say anything. I'd never met a famous person before. This was the best footballer in the world, the person I now wanted to be when I grew up, *talking to me*. It was amazing. It was like a dream, like I wasn't really there.

He played for West Ham United. Dad told me he was also their captain. From that day, I became their biggest supporter. I spent all my pocket money on anything in their colours of claret and blue and decorated my room with posters and cuttings of all the players.

Bobby was known as the 'gentleman of football'. He was always well dressed, polite and hardly ever got booked on the pitch. Every single night after school I went over to the park, just like him with my jersey tucked neatly into my shorts, and practised my football skills, pretending to be him with every tackle and pass until it was too dark to see the ball anymore.

Only then would I go back home, though I would immediately ask if I could wait up to watch him on *Match of the Day* on TV.

Bobby Moore OBE is widely regarded as one of the greatest football players of all time and is cited by Pele as the greatest defender that he ever played against. He most notably played for West Ham United, captaining the club for more than ten years. This extract is from Matt Dickinson's biography *Bobby Moore: The Man in Full.*

Like mother like son. Into this tidy home came an excessively neat child. Even as a youngster, Bobby laid down strict rules about his clothes. Shirts must never be folded; they must be placed on hangers and hung from the picture rail around the sitting room. He would take them upstairs to his wardrobe and place them in order, dark to light, like a filing system. A peculiar habit for a boy.

Perfectionism became a defining Moore characteristic and with it a hatred of being shown up. Moore always recalled that his worst day at school was the time he was ordered to go up in front of his classmates and sing 'God Save the Queen'. He was mortified and the words came out in a half-hearted drone. Talking about it years later, he could still feel the hot flush of embarrassment.

Cause: perfectionist public figures

As small children the only people who affect how we really feel about ourselves are the ones we personally know – family, friends, teachers and so on. But as we grow, our world grows, to include other people we look up to, who can influence how we view ourselves and how we want to be.

Many well-known artists, record breaking sportsman, charity campaigners and global politicians are driven by the need to be perfect, to always be right, to hide their flaws and never admit when they are wrong.

But social media has widened the circle of people we can admire to also include those who have achieved little, except to present us with an impossibly perfect image of themselves and their life.

We now compare our own lives and happiness, not only with those of friends, family and heroes, but also with the richest and most famous people on earth. And there's no way that anyone can feel good enough after doing that.

In many cases, the biggest, best-known social media 'stars' are perfectionists themselves because, exactly like us, they recognize curating a perfect online persona potentially provides them with an opportunity to prove to others that they are leading a perfect life. Like us, they crave 'likes' and admiration, but for them even more so, because they have discovered, as all perfectionists who have any success discover, that fame and fortune do not bring the contentment they expected. They still need us to 'like' their life for them to feel worthy. And they can only achieve that by making the rest of us feel unworthy, jealous and fearful that we are missing out (FOMO). They can make people believe they are missing out on happiness and contentment itself.

We can be happy with our simple lives, with our friends and family, but they teach us that that isn't enough. We should have more – more stuff, more success, more money – an unattainable more.

But often these well-known perfectionists only share half their life. Very few share the stresses, sacrifices, broken relationships and loneliness that surround them – the things that would spoil and tarnish that 'perfect' image they have so carefully constructed.

We can enjoy and admire their work, but we should not put them on a pedestal. After all, we don't know what's behind the camera, out of our sight.

What can parents do against the tsunami of children's heroes sharing their perfectly curated lives? Discuss with your child what's outside the frame of that perfect picture. This is the side a few heroes have started to share in biographies and blog posts – the painful and often lonely side, the mental health problems they have suffered. Reality.

The reality of how the modern world makes many of us feel. Even our heroes.

AGE 8
Doing what you're told

At home, we had (unwritten) punishments if we didn't do as we were told and rewards if we were good. I was as good as I could be, though I never quite lived up to my parents' expectations to be as 'good as gold'.

If I was bad ...
I was sent to my bedroom.
If it was quite bad, without tea.
If it was really bad, with a smack on my legs.
I wasn't allowed out after tea.
I had to go to bed early.
Dad would tell me off.
I would feel bad all day.
I felt unloved, lonely, sad.

If I was good ...
Dad would read me a bedtime story.
I could stay out till it got dark.
Dad would help me with my homework.
Dad wouldn't shout at me.
Dad wouldn't call me lazy.
I wouldn't feel bad all day.
I felt safe, loved and happy

Brian Wilson is a singer-songwriter, producer and co-founder of the Beach Boys. He has written more than 25 top-40 hits and two of the most innovative and iconic albums of all time, *Pet Sounds* and *Smile.*

As he peaked creatively, his mental health deteriorated and his contributions to the band diminished. He became a recluse and substance abuser, while being 'controlled' by a psychologist. It took a court order to enable him to 'escape' and begin the journey to recovery and once again to be happy and contented.

He has said about his father, 'He taught me how to be a perfectionist.' and writes about his relationship with him in his autobiography *I am Brian Wilson.*

The more I thought about it, the more I felt sad, too, because thinking about my childhood in Hawthorne made me think about my Dad. Thinking about my Dad was the big can of worms. I started young and I got older, but he stayed one of the most important people in my life, in good ways and bad. He could be generous and guide me towards great things, but he could also be brutal and belittle me and sometimes even make me regret that I was alive.

I learnt all those things when I was too young to understand them. Maybe they are the kind of things that you're never supposed to understand. .

Cause: conditional love

All children need rules to grow up with, but we shouldn't ever let them believe, even for a moment, that a parent's love for them is dependent on how well they abide by them.

A child believing their parents' love is conditional on their behaviour or performance only leads to a lack of self-confidence and long-term mental health problems: the message they receive when they hear 'That wasn't good enough' starts to morph into 'You aren't good enough', and they go on to dedicate their lives to trying to achieve the perfection they mistakenly believe their parents require if they are to give them their love.

Many perfectionist adults recall feeling, from a very young age, that they needed to be a perfectly obedient child. The 'demand' laid on them as children to follow the rules has developed into an adult obsession.

Many perfectionist adults, aware that their feelings of needing to prove themselves 'good enough' often stem from a relationship with one or more important adults from their childhood, will recall the interactions they had with these significant people when they have to decide their own response to similar moments when they occur in their own adult life. Each decision they make needs to be perfect, so that it leads to the belief that the person from their childhood would be impressed enough to acknowledge that they were in fact 'good enough'.

That's the daily decision process a perfectionist can go through.

This process can often take place when difficult moments arise during parenting their own children and they have to decide between repeating the (disliked) actions of adults they loved from their own childhood, or distancing themselves from it, by making their own judgement.

If this moment arises, give yourself time to make your own decision. Follow what your heart says (nature), rather than automatically repeat any disliked habits from your own childhood (nurture).

AGE 9
Just the way it is

Dad's Mum and Dad lived near us. We called them 'mini Grandma and Grandad' because they had a Mini car, while Mum's parents, who lived near the sea, were called 'bungalow Grandma and Grandad' because, well, they lived in a bungalow. We would visit both sets of grandparents often, and I loved it. They would spoil us rotten, more than Mum and Dad ever did.

Mini Grandma and Grandad were most like Mum and Dad. When we went around their small two-up two-down home, Dad's Dad would be working away in his shed, busy making something, while Grandma was always in the kitchen 'putting the kettle on'.

Bungalow Grandad managed a shop, which was exciting, and I thought they were rich because they lived at the seaside. We loved staying with them – being taken to the seaside and treated with ice cream every day, what wasn't to love? One day they moved from the seaside to live nearer us, which was great because we got to see them even more often. Every time we went around after school Bungalow Grandad would take us to the shops, where we got to choose more sweets than we were ever normally allowed, and he got to smoke a cigarette, which he told us not to ever tell Grandma about.

We were aware he wasn't very well – he had a bad cough – but one day Mum called us into the kitchen to tell us Grandad had just died from cancer. From that day onwards, we never saw bungalow Grandma again. Ever. We weren't told why. We overheard an argument but it was something between Mum and Grandma and nothing to do with us, we were only nine, seven and three years old. We just did what we were told.

We didn't go to Grandad's funeral.

We never saw or heard from Grandma ever again.

Cause: traumatic incidents in childhood

Traumatic incidents involving important relationships with adults are the most recognized cause of perfectionism – it could be abuse, death, serious ongoing parental arguments, bullying, parents separating, a parent leaving home and so on. This is because the child can, in some mistaken way, blame themselves for the incident and any consequences.

They can go on to feel they might be able to repair everything or see more of someone important they lose touch with, by being as perfect as they possibly can, in everything they do. They try to please everyone. They try to make everyone happy.

It can be the start of a lifetime's belief that love obviously isn't enough to keep things 'good' but being perfect could be the answer. It's the only way they could possibly make everything 'right' again.

Many of the world's top athletes and sport stars have suffered traumatic incidents in childhood, including many Olympic medal-winning athletes growing up in homes in which their father has left while they were still at a young age. The simple, win-or-lose scenario of competitive sport appears to offer genuine opportunities to achieve a moment of perfection. Not to prove they are number one but to make their life right again.

Sir Bradley Wiggins CBE is one of Britain's greatest ever cyclists. He is the only professional to have won both the World and Olympic championships on the track and road, as well as winning the Tour de France and holding the iconic track hour record. The son of the Australian cyclist Gary Wiggins, he was born to a British mother in Ghent, Belgium, and raised in London from the age of two. His wife Cath has spoken about the two Bradleys in her life. 'There is the loving, kind, patient husband and father who occasionally makes an appearance at home, but then there is the selfish, inconsiderate, driven, perfectionist of a professional cyclist.'

Below is an extract from his autobiography, *My Time*, about his own traumatic childhood.

George had always been there. He was the father figure, the role model in my young life, from the day when my mother Linda and I moved into my nan and grandads flat in Kilburn after my father Gary had walked out on us. Gary didn't so much walk out on us in Christmas 1982 as throw us out. I wasn't even two years old. We'd gone from our home in Ghent to see my mum's parents and he called my mum to say she and I weren't to come back to Belgium. He'd got together with someone else.

For my first eight or nine years I spent a lot of time with George so he was like a father in many respects; he bought me up. He had been to watch Gary Wiggins race when he was with my mum. Gary was a hard-drinking Australian bike racer who'd come over to Belgium to make a living competing on the track in the six days in the winter and the Kermesses – the little circuit races that make up the bulk of the Belgium calendar – through the summer. George would tell me about a time when Gary had crashed somewhere and pulled all the splinters from the wooden track out of his back with Pliers.

Gary shut us out of his life from before I was two until I was in my seventeenth year, from the day he came back to London with four black bin liners containing our stuff from Belgium and dumped them at the bottom of stairs to the flat when Nan and Granddad George lived. He moved to Australia later, and briefly, in my late teens we spent a little time together there, but we never built a proper relationship.

Gary had used amphetamines to race; he'd sold them to other bike riders and worst of all he'd knocked my mum about. In spite of all that, George never, ever said to me what he thought of my dad until I was about 18 or 19, and he told me, 'look he's a wanker...'. I suppose he left me to find out in my own way what kind of a person Gary was. I do know however, that from the point of view of a father, he never forgave Gary for what he did to us.

AGE 10
The best days ...?

Just as I liked nursery, I really enjoyed school. I had a good time, making things and still simply playing with my friends.

... Until that is, about the third year, when I was 'instructed', in no uncertain terms, that I was now too old to wear shorts and spend every break time playing football. From now on I was to wear a shirt and tie and spend every break time revising for tests on Tudor history, weathering and erosion, or Pythagoras' theorem.

From that moment, I stopped enjoying school.

I couldn't. I wanted to be outside playing or making things, not sitting at a desk. I couldn't justify to myself why I needed to learn half the things that teachers were trying to teach me. When was I ever going to need to know this stuff? The more they told me, the less I heard.

I had once loved school but by then I didn't even want to go anymore.

That just resulted in too many times when test results were read out to the class and I would be bottom, and made fun of, as much by the teachers as by the other kids. If I did badly, I was made to stand on my chair in front of everyone.

One day we had to write a school report – on ourselves.

The next day the teacher announced to the class, 'Christopher will now stand up and read his "report" to you all.'

Nice.

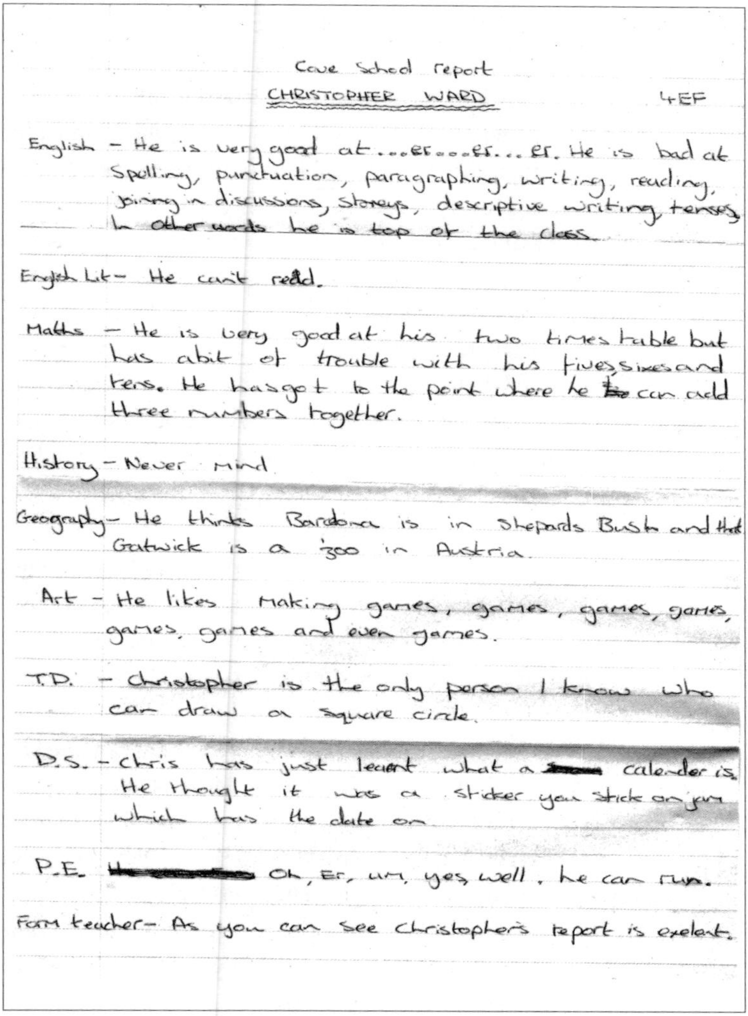

Cove School report

CHRISTOPHER WARD 4EF

English – He is very good at....er....er....er. He is bad at Spelling, punctuation, paragraphing, writing, reading, joining in discussions, storeys, descriptive writing, tenses. In other words he is top of the class.

English Lit – He can't read.

Maths – He is very good at his two times table but has abit of trouble with his fives, sixes and tens. He has got to the point where he can add three numbers together.

History – Never mind

Geography – He thinks Barcelona is in Shepards Bush and that Gatwick is a zoo in Austria.

Art – He likes making games, games, games, games, games, games and even games.

T.D. – Christopher is the only person I know who can draw a square circle.

D.S. – Chris has just learnt what a [redacted] calender is. He thought it was a sticker you stick on jam which has the date on.

P.E. [redacted] Oh, er, um, yes well, he can run.

Form teacher – As you can see Christopher's report is exelent.

The school report I wrote on myself

Cause: academic pressure

The constant pressure to have to achieve academically is one of the key reasons we now have an epidemic of perfectionism.

Teachers are required to demand the very highest standards from children, in eight different subjects, for six hours of every day, for five days of every week, for thirteen years. While at home, most parents, having been raised with the same ethos, consider the demands simply a normal requirement of school life and instruct their children to 'just get on with it'.

Children are taught from a young age to compete with each other to be top of their class. Only then, they are informed, will their parents be proud of them, will their careers be good enough, will they be happy. For those thirty school hours a week, children are learning that judging and competing with their friends and colleagues is the norm for our society.

Even when they do succeed, in response, teachers will often raise their expectation levels even higher. So, what was previously considered successful becomes their new 'normal', keeping stress levels high and confidence levels low. And if they do struggle, in response, teachers often refuse to lower their expectation levels. So, what was previously considered achievable becomes their new 'impossible', again, keeping stress levels high and confidence levels low.

Children can only be a 'high' achiever in their class if one of their friends or colleagues is a 'low' achiever. They can only feel good about themselves if one of their classmates feels bad.

So many return home with confidence levels low, to find, not fully supportive parents, but ones distracted by their own demands of work or need to escape them, via the screen of a mobile phone.

It is impossible for this scenario to not result in many children growing into adults who have an overriding gut feeling they are just not good enough.

The education system needs a complete overhaul, so that children are taught to act as collaborative individuals, supporting and working together to enhance each other's strengths, and not all measured under the same competitive criteria. Unfortunately, this is unlikely to happen anytime soon.

So, how can children feel good enough in front of their friends, teachers, family and the mirror in their bathroom?

They need to be taught that they are good enough *as they are.* Doing well in one subject won't make them a successful person, just as much as not doing so well in another won't result in them becoming a failure. Which is, unfortunately, how many currently feel.

If there is one critical lesson they should take from their entire schooling, it is that academic achievement will rarely dictate their future, but their ability to get on and be able to collaborate with anyone will.

Ann Mroz is the editor and director of the *TES* (formally, *Times Educational Supplement*). Here she talks about the culture of perfectionism in our schools:

In our society, we have no truck with those we perceive to be wrong, we give no leeway for imperfection, there are no excuses; we have time only for perfection and we fetishise success, which is often presented as an airbrushed, varnished version of events. It is unachievable – but falling short is not tolerated.

This extends into our schools. The culture of hyper-accountability leads to an unhealthy push for that perfection that permeates through leadership, through teachers (it's not good for them either) and down to students.

Out of school, young people know that they are going to be judged on their appearance. In school, they know that everything rests on their grades.

Sir Al Aynsley-Green is the former Children's Commissioner for England. The following is an extract from his book *The British Betrayal of Childhood.* (2018):

Childhood is being ruined in the UK, and the education system is largely to blame. The consequences of cutting budgets, the narrow test-oriented curriculum, the denial of the importance of the arts, the failure to see the need for technical qualifications to meet our skills shortages and the rhetoric of 'choice', when for most families this is an impossible dream, all point to a disconnect with what actually matters to families.

Similarly, children with mental health issues are being neglected. The bar for access to Camhs (funded support) is so high, many children can't access it. We're seeing the endpoint of at least twenty years of denial of the importance of emotional ill health in children. Meanwhile, teachers are being forced to witness children suffering without help. It's appalling.

AGE 11
Trying your best

Regularly finishing bottom of the class meant that I struggled to generate any enthusiasm to do my homework. Instead, I channelled it all towards becoming a professional footballer like my hero, Bobby Moore. I still used to practise, hour upon hour on my own, in front of our house, until it was too dark to see the ball anymore. 'If you put as much effort into your homework as practising football, you'd be top of the class' was a line I heard regularly from my parents, as I trudged tiredly, through the front door.

But that's not what the cool boys, who were good at football and got to pick the teams for games, thought. They considered my performance in classrooms the indicator by which they should judge my performance on the football pitch. So, being better at football than schoolwork meant nothing when we had to stand against a wall waiting for one of them to pick us for their team. I was always picked second to last, just ahead of the boy with a dodgy leg.

Despite the weekly humiliation, I didn't give up and eventually they couldn't ignore me anymore and I got to make it to the edge of success – to the edge of the football pitch, to be exact, standing on the touchline, freezing cold, as a substitute, for the school team.

If I did ever get on the actual pitch, it was normally to play at right-back. 'Right back behind the goal', as the playground joke went. Once, I got picked to play centre-forward, but after just ten minutes, the manager, an overenthusiastic, win-at-all-odds dad, substituted me. So, head bowed, I walked slowly off. My dad loomed over me as I sat on the turf and took off my boots, really trying not to cry. The other team's manager asked if there was anything wrong. After I replied there wasn't, he said I could play for them if I wanted. He was just being nice.

In another match, just after half-time our goalkeeper felt sick, so I volunteered to go in goal. Obviously, I gave it everything, diving all over the place, and I made some good saves. The final result was 0–15. But I only let in four of them.

I remember every embarrassing moment.

I felt useless. There were 120 boys in my school year. No one ever said, 'Well done, you are the twelfth best footballer in your year. You're in the top 10 per cent. of footballers for your age.' No one ever said anything like that. They just said, 'You're substitute today', and at the end of the match came the inevitable: 'Sorry, you didn't get a game. See you next week.'

Being a footballer was my dream but I began to realize I wasn't good enough to make it come true. I started to come in from practising before it got dark or not even go out at all, preferring to just go upstairs and spend more time in my bedroom instead.

Consequence: the belief 'I'm not good enough'

Children are constantly told 'You can only do your best', which is true. But if they believe they have done that, but the result is not a fair representation for the effort they put in, that can lead either to a supportive conversation with teachers and/or a loving evening with understanding parents, or to the belief that, if what they did is not good enough, that must mean they are not good enough.

It can result in perfectionism.

Adults that manage children's activities should be aware of the lifelong impact each decision they make can have on a child's confidence, both negative and positive. All they have to do to make it a positive experience is prioritize the children and not the outcome.

AGE 12
Behind the bedroom door
Escaping the demands of perfectionism (1)

I gradually let myself become invisible at school, which was difficult when I was always standing on my chair because I was bottom of the class, at the side of football pitches because I was the substitute, or by the wall because I was a blushing wallflower around girls. But ask my classmates now and not many of them will remember I actually sat next to them, in the same classrooms, for 'the best years of our life'.

I turned up on time, did my homework, just about on time. I didn't get into any good books but neither did I get into the bad ones. I just retreated behind my, firmly shut, bedroom door. The only place where I could escape being judged all the time, where ... I could be ME!

Behind that door I was free. Free to do whatever I wanted and play loud music! Or at least until Mum shouted up for me to 'Turn that down ... and tidy your room.' I could escape having to help Dad with something I couldn't do or trying to revise for something I knew I couldn't learn.

In my bedroom, no one could give me low marks, tell me off, not pick me or pick on me.

I was in a world of my very own. Reading pop magazines, listening to the music I had started buying with my paper-round money, trying to complete football sticker albums, making scrapbooks and listening to F1 races on the radio. I was living my life through magazines, rather than in the kitchen, classroom and alongside football pitches. I spent less time communicating with people I knew and more time following the lives of people I didn't.

And I started to spend hour upon hour doing something I loved: inventing games and making them up as if they were good enough to buy. My bedroom floor was covered with drawn-up plans, dice, counters, rules, rules and more rules, and discarded sheets of sticky-backed plastic.

When I eventually deemed the games were good enough to play with the rest of the family, they said I should send them to the big game companies, to see if they wanted to make 'proper' versions that people could buy in actual shops. I never did. As if my games were going to be good enough for that?

Instead, I used all the materials to make Christmas presents for the rest of the family. I wanted to give brilliant presents to everyone. I preferred giving presents to receiving them. I liked the idea of the family liking my homemade gifts more than I liked the idea of receiving the gifts they bought me. That may have been because I never held out much hope that I would be opening a present I actually ever really, really wanted. It was tough, putting on a happy face, at the sight of a gift that wasn't quite what I'd hoped for or wanted.

It wasn't clever or sporty, but I loved every moment in my bedroom and inventing those games. I was in a place I controlled, doing something I could perfect, to my heart's content.

People seemed to love the results but it would have been embarrassing if they knew how much I worked on and cared about making those games – how often I made and remade pieces, wrote and rewrote the rules – all in pursuit of creating a game they would actually think was all right, and not just pretend they did.

Escaping the demands of perfectionism (1)

Perfectionists need a 'third space'. Somewhere they can disappear, to escape the nonstop demand they feel for everything to be just right during the day and at home. A space where they can take a break from trying to have perfect interactions with everyone and escape the expectations they believe everyone has of them.

Initially, this space is often a bedroom, into which the teenager disappears in order to escape any (perceived) demands from parents, teachers and peers. Nowadays, however, the bedroom, like every other place, has been invaded by social media and is no longer a safe, private haven.

Other popular 'third spaces' include coffee shops, gyms and the roads, pools and parks where they undertake solo sporting pursuits, such as cycling, swimming and running. These are places and pursuits where they can be alone and in control, but also still surrounded by others and therefore not lonely.

A third space is where the perfectionist can get their 'head together', before once again entering the uncontrollable world around them. However small it is, wherever it is, perfectionists best survive the day-to-day, by having such a place to escape.

Don't take it as rudeness if a perfectionist partner or child chooses time on their own in preference to time with you. Sometimes they just need it, to reset themselves.

AGE 13
Sorry

It was a sunny Sunday morning, just after my paper round. I remember every tiny detail clearly.

I had waited until Mum and Dad were in the kitchen, then I sneaked out of my bedroom, down the stairs and out the front door. I was scared. I ran as fast as possible, until I was out of sight of the house and then continued to walk quickly to the train station and just got on the first train. It happened to be going to London.

An hour earlier both Mum and Dad had been in my bedroom. They had just found the newspapers I had stolen from my paper round. As they demanded answers, I felt ashamed but I was also embarrassed. I only wanted them so I could have the football match reports from every paper because, childishly – or so it sounded when I said it out loud – I wanted 'my football scrapbook to be the best'.

So, when I slipped the papers in my bag, I sort of thought it was OK. Other kids at school were daily nicking half the contents of the local newsagents. I could never do that, but I did want to be a little more rebellious, like everyone else. The fact I'd only taken a few newspapers didn't make any difference to the way I felt then, though.

Once the train reached Waterloo Station, I just sat on the platform for what felt like hours, not knowing what to do. I was thirteen, sitting in the middle of London, on my own, miles from home, nervous, a little scared, embarrassed and ashamed. I'd been caught stealing and for a childish reason as well.

I couldn't have stayed at home though. If my parents loved me when I was good and I had been as bad as I thought I could be in their eyes, how disappointed in me would they be? It was made very clear what was right and wrong, there was never any doubt about where the line was. I had definitely crossed it.

Eventually, I nervously made myself phone home. Dad answered, 'I'm at Waterloo Station ... if you love me,' I said quickly, before putting the phone down and bursting into tears.

I didn't move. A man asked if I was OK at one point. After about two hours, I saw Dad walking towards me. I bowed my head in shame. 'You're all right then?' he said, as if it was no big deal. I walked with him to the car and we drove home, without another word being spoken.

Mum told me I had scared them both to death and not to do it again, ever. As always, I did what I was told.

Cause: embarrassment and shame

In our highly competitive world of comparison and judgements, for a young child, feeling embarrassed or ashamed, for whatever reason – a bad school report, caught doing something wrong, thinking they have no friends or not living up to expected norms in some way – can quickly lead to solitude, loneliness, lack of confidence and anxiety. They can start to genuinely feel that it may now be impossible to ever be good enough, for anyone.

If you notice any change in behaviour of a child – a lessening of confidence and an increasing amount of time spent behind a closed bedroom door, for instance – try to instigate an honest conversation and offer support and unconditional love.

If they do something wrong, they should know that they may be punished, but also that that bears no relevance to how they are loved.

Children need to understand they are always good enough, always loved.

This innate need to feel loved does not miraculously disappear when they grow up.

AGE 14
Thatcher's children

Dad always worked long days. Mum worked two jobs: typist during the day, office cleaner during the evenings. They worked hard for every penny they spent on us. I knew that because they'd often tell us it was the case. They didn't get much reward other than seeing us fed, clothed and appreciative. Like most parents of teenagers, they often didn't get the appreciation.

Then, along came their perfect politician, Margaret Thatcher. She won elections, first to lead the Conservative Party and then the whole of Britain. And as the newly elected prime minister, she promised to reward them and everyone else who worked hard.

She promised that they would get paid more, be able to buy more, that their homes and cars would get bigger, that they could become successful enough that they would eventually be able to retire happy. They would have earned it.

Britons bought into this philosophy and voted for her in record numbers.

My father didn't just look like her Conservative minister Norman Tebbit, he agreed with him: many people were just lazy and, if they wanted to do well and get a job, they should just get on their bike and keep cycling until they found one.

And that's the way we were raised, as 'Thatcher's children'. It was instilled in us. if we worked harder, we would earn more money, be able to buy more things, be more successful and, ultimately, therefore be happier.

Simple.

The following is an extract from 'Perfectionism is Increasing over Time: A Meta-Analysis of Birth Cohort Differences from 1989 to 2016', a study by Thomas Curran of the University of Bath and Andrew P. Hill of York St John University.

Across many western societies, today's young people are the first generation to grow up in a society based on the principles of neoliberalism, championed by the leaders of the late 20th century, Ronald Reagan and Margaret Thatcher. Over the last 50 years, communal interest and civic responsibility have been progressively eroded, replaced by a focus on self-interest and competition in a supposedly free and open market place.

In this new market-based society, young people were evaluated in a host of new ways. School and university testing, job performance assessments (and now social media) mean young people could be sifted, sorted and ranked by peers, teachers and employers. If young people rank poorly, the logic of our market-based society dictates that they are less deserving, that their inferiority reflects some personal weakness or flaw.

Cause: neoliberalism

If becoming successful is the only way a perfectionist believes they can prove themselves 'good enough', then they will also truly believe that only by significant achievement can they even start to consider they can be happy. They believe they need to earn their happiness, that they can only feel it, if they deserve to. That it's not a natural human state, but something you can only genuinely feel if you achieve.

Neoliberalism, already long pervasive throughout business, is now rampant throughout society, in the age of the internet, and is an underlying cause of anxiety among perfectionists.

The global technology and social media businesses create their own success by allowing their platforms to be used to sell us fake/curated, perfect success. At the same time, they have made that vision of success – as defined by their own global terms – almost impossible for any individual to achieve, certainly not to a sufficient extent for them ever to feel happy and contented.

In fact, the self-same neoliberal values that have enabled these giants to become unregulated, untaxed superpowers mean that many people now even struggle to afford day-to-day life, as jobs, benefits and lifelong careers disappear, along with any chance of success and happiness.

The values of neoliberalism lead many perfectionists closer to the edge of a mental health issue than to success.

But... success is for business or sport. Happiness and contentment are not achieved by success, but by understanding why you are trying to achieve it. That understanding alone can bring an end to the lifelong chase after the impossible.

AGE 15
Can always do better

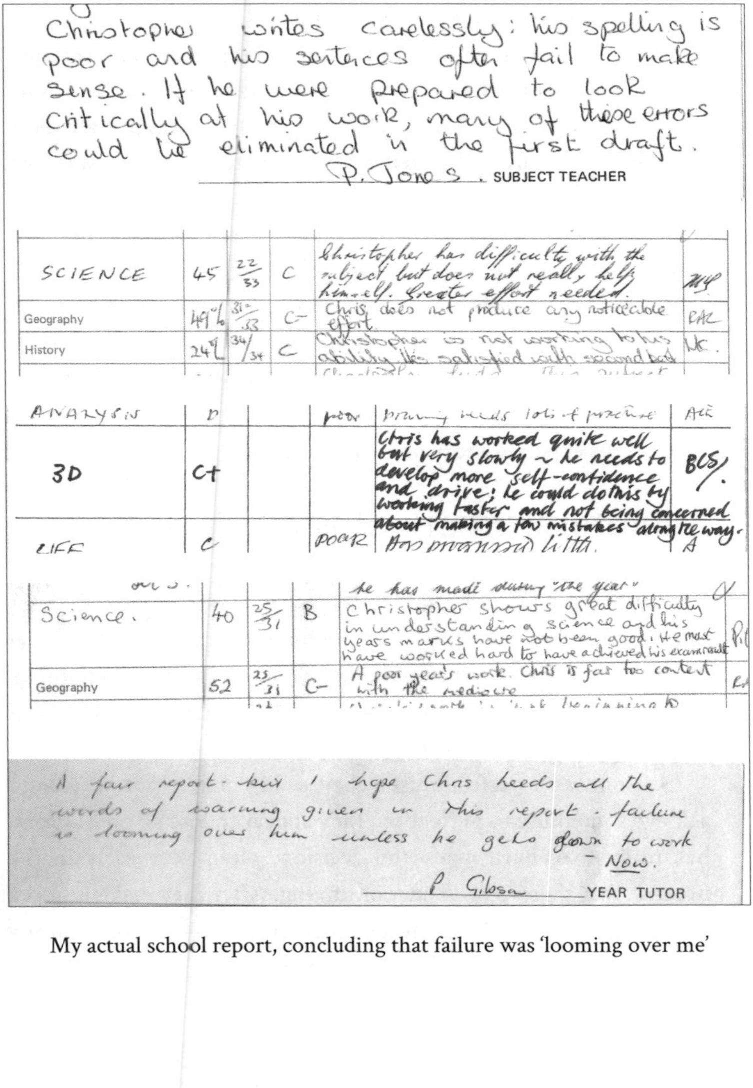

Christopher writes carelessly: his spelling is poor and his sentences often fail to make sense. If he were prepared to look critically at his work, many of these errors could be eliminated in the first draft.

P. Jones SUBJECT TEACHER

SCIENCE	45	22/33	C	Christopher has difficulty with the subject but does not really help himself. Greater effort needed.	[illegible]
Geography	49%	31/33	C–	Chris does not produce any noticeable effort.	RAC
History	24%	34/34	C	Christopher is not working to his ability. He's satisfied with second best	NC.

ANALYSIS	D			poor	Drawing needs lots of practice	Ach
3D	C+				Chris has worked quite well but very slowly – he needs to develop more self-confidence and drive; he could do this by working faster and not being concerned about making a few mistakes along the way.	BCS/.
LIFE	C			POOR	Has progressed little.	A

				he has made during the year"	
Science.	40	25/31	B	Christopher shows great difficulty in understanding science and his years marks have not been good. He must have worked hard to have achieved his exam result	Pi
Geography	52	23/31	C–	A poor year's work. Chris is far too content with the mediocre	R

A fair report - but I hope Chris heeds all the words of warning given in this report - failure is looming over him unless he gets down to work - Now.

P Gibson YEAR TUTOR

My actual school report, concluding that failure was 'looming over me'

Two years after having to write my own school report, I got the real one from my teachers. I hadn't started trying harder, despite the promise of success and happiness. My earlier one had been uncannily accurate.

At least my teacher didn't make me read this one out to the whole class. My parents read it out to me, though.

I had found school tough. I went through the motions but I certainly wasn't engaged. My teachers thought I was a waste of time. My results were terrible. Apparently, I could always do better. I was just a useless, uneducated idiot really. I'd wasted every opportunity, or so I was told. Repeatedly.

I pretty much failed all my exams, apart from Art, and that was because of the games I'd loved making in my bedroom.

With the dreams of being a professional sportsman or inventor of games well gone, the height of my career ambition was to go on to the local sixth-form college and then, if things went well, get some sort of local job.

My parents expected more of me than this.

Symptom: 'all or nothing' thinking

Perfectionists approach things with 'all or nothing' thinking. If they think they won't be able to achieve something perfectly, they often won't even try. They view anything other than perfection as failure, so the fear of public humiliation causes them to do nothing. Achieving some improvement is still considered failure. Success is the only option: if you don't succeed, you are a failure.

As soon as a perfectionist believes they might not be able to achieve something to perfection, they appear to lose all enthusiasm, but really they have made the decision, often very early in the process, that there is no point continuing. After they make it, it is a chore to get them to finish the job to any reasonable standard, in any reasonable timeframe, or even to finish it at all.

It is generally thought that this behaviour is simply a result of someone becoming bored quickly, and always wanting to move on to something else. Perfectionists are not bored; they just know that, if they continue, people will not be impressed enough for them to feel worthy. So, there is literally no point finishing it. They would have publicly failed, so, fairly they conclude, it makes more sense to not even try in the first place.

It's all or nothing. Improvement is not a good enough reason to do anything.

The other side of the coin is, while they still believe in a project, and in themselves to deliver it perfectly, they can become obsessed and often continue tasks way beyond when they have stopped being productive.

Perfectionists will also take their choice of words, opinions and behaviour to what we would consider extreme lengths, to make something perfect. They, on the other hand, will not view any of it as extreme but simply very normal and therefore often fail to understand if anyone has a problem with their approach.

We need to help the perfectionist believe that there is value in persevering, to make the thing they are doing, not perfect, but just better. That people will not think they are a failure if they just improve.

If society makes the effort to gain a real understanding of perfectionism, it will be able to provide proper support to those who struggle with the condition and unable them to just get on with *improving*.

It's only now, after a lifetime believing I was doomed to be a failure that I understand I wasn't useless at school. I'm not stupid. I had just given up trying, I knew I could never make my schoolwork perfect or even good enough, so I stopped trying. And for that I was branded a failure.

AGE 16
Everyone's laughing at you

So, I wasn't clever with my mind, practical with my hands or skilful with my feet, and I certainly wasn't as 'manly' as my dad, or, as it turned out, even other boys. There was only one option left, I became a geek.

My bedroom became a flight deck for my fantasy world. I devoured science-fiction magazines, TV series and movies, and lost myself on other planets. I loved them more than my own.

Somehow, back on Planet Earth, I got into an art college. I had no qualifications but I had the games. As it turned out, they were just enough to get me in. Now I could get to spend all day making things, rather than wasting all day learning things. I couldn't draw or paint, or write or add up, so it was amazing I was offered a place, at a real-life art college, full of overconfident, too-good-looking teenagers.

My lack of self-confidence, which even my teachers had noted in my school reports, didn't stop me really wanting to have a girlfriend, though – just someone who was pretty and into music and *Star Wars*; someone I could just share my real loves and fantasy worlds with.

I had fancied a few girls, either at school or on the checkouts at the supermarket, where I was working evenings collecting trolleys. I felt too boring to ask any of them out, I just hoped it would sort of just happen. There were so many different emotions going on inside my head but I didn't share anything with anyone, apart from my diary. I wasn't one for sharing many, if any, secret pubescent thoughts even with my diary though. This is the turbulent emotional journey I went on, precisely recorded as a list of facts and stats, when I worked alongside a girl at the supermarket, who I liked ...

Wednesday
In the evening I went to do my part-time job at Sainsbury's. I was on trolleys with David and Dave. They tried chatting up Betty.

Thursday
Me, Dave and David discussed Betty. For dinner I had mince and for pudding plums.

I watched television and listened to my radio but I couldn't help thinking about Betty. I was thinking of asking her skateboarding on Saturday.

Saturday
For dinner I had fishfingers and for pudding tinned peaches.
In the evening I watched television.

Monday
In the evening I went to work at Sainsbury's. I was on trolleys.
I walked halfway home with Betty.

Thursday
Betty was working on the door which was pretty good so I tried chatting her up. At 8:30 p.m. I mucked around with her and David and his CB radio.

Saturday
In the afternoon I went round Betty's house to lend her some records I bought. I talked to her for half an hour then I came home and continued cleaning my room.

Friday
After work, I organised my birthday party. People began to arrive at 8 p.m. In the end there were 8 girls and 16 boys. I wanted Betty to come but she couldn't but she sent a card. It has lots of love and kisses written at the bottom.

Saturday
I asked Betty to a party tonight. She said she would come if she's not going out. I then listened to my records after a hair wash and bath.

In the evening I went to the party, at the Railway Enthusiasts Club. On my own.

extracts from my diary

In my mind, and my diary, I had a whole relationship with someone while sharing zero emotions with her or my diary – and without her being in the slightest bit aware it had even happened. I had more chance of managing a Sainsbury's than going out with Betty who worked on the checkout.

I did actually ask a girl to dance once. She looked nice. She was chatting to her friends. She just said 'no'. That was it. One girl, one night. She hardly even glanced at me. She might well have not even heard me. But those two seconds reinforced my negative self-image and I never asked a girl to dance again. Until my wedding day.

When you're a geeky teenager it doesn't take much to break even the modicum of self-confidence you might have regarding relationships. On top of not being good academically, it became clear to me that I was not good-looking either. I started to worry about my hair, what I wore, the spots on my face.

Never asking a girl to dance was OK, because dancing is still the last thing in the world I like doing. But I don't think I've asked another girl out ever either, which has been a lot less OK. All I wanted was to be loved by someone for whom I really was.

I couldn't tell anyone I liked them as it would have made me too vulnerable. I believed they would most likely reject my advance, publicly. The shame would be too much.

Instead of sharing my emotions I started to bury them. The person sharing how they felt, wasn't speaking for the person inside. I was faking emotions that if I didn't display would have made me appear cold-hearted. But I couldn't let myself actually feel them, I couldn't be that vulnerable.

Consequence: feeling judged, too scared to try anything

The demand for perfection can be transmitted in tiny ways, some as silent as a raised eyebrow over a B grade rather than an A or even a simple 'no' when you ask a girl to dance. Perfectionism often develops while the person is single, and therefore the perfectionist's symptoms can become totally entrenched, making it very hard for him or her to make any of the compromises that a happy and fulfilling relationship requires.

Social media consequences

It was hard enough navigating relationships when I was growing up but it is even more fraught now, in our online world. Today's teenagers are foot soldiers, at the forefront of the world of critical judgement we have created. They are on the front line, getting shot down if what they do, what they wear, what they look like, what they attempt, if who they are even, is not considered good enough. And social media is the messenger that can inform their whole world in a split second.

Perfectionism is the trait they develop to hide their vulnerability. An early sign it is taking hold can be the creating, deleting and re-editing of social media posts before actually sharing them. Every single one has to be perfect, or appear to be so, to avoid any public humiliation.

So how do we combat this? Limiting a child's online usage when they actively use it for all their communication is the wrong approach, even if it wasn't impossible. What you can do, however, is try to limit their passive following of other people's lives – especially people they don't know and people who foster their own curated perfection on their followers; celebrities and the like. They should be encouraged to use their smartphone and social media to communicate and share with people they know (people they've actually met) and not to 'follow' those they don't.

If you are to achieve that, they will need something else they want to do instead with their time. You need to spend your time helping them find a way to stop wasting theirs. Find out what that could be and help them do it. Spending more time doing enjoyable things with you might be near the top of the list.

The online epidemic of children being scared to share anything but perfection on social media is increasingly being replicated in real life too. Offline, children can be obsessed with getting their schoolwork or hobbies 'just right' before they will share with anyone, refusing to enter competitions or even attend after-school classes because they believe they are not perfect, and therefore it would literally be too embarrassing to try. This is particularly the case when a video of a failed attempt can be instantly shared with everyone they know, just with the touch of a key.

If you are concerned your child is displaying these traits, continue to show them your unconditional love and support, encourage honest and open conversations about their feelings, but also consider either them or both of you speaking to a mental health specialist.

Here the ex-Facebook president **Sean Parker** talks about how social media is manipulating everyone to feel less validated:

When Facebook was being developed the objective was, how do we consume as much of your time and conscious attention as possible? It was this mindset that led to the creation of features such as the 'like' button that would give users a little dopamine hit, to encourage them to upload more content.

It's a social-validation feedback loop, exactly the kind of thing that a hacker like myself would come up with, because you're exploiting a vulnerability in human psychology.

When a network grows to have more than 2 billion users, it literally changes your relationship with society, with each other. It probably interferes with productivity in weird ways. God only knows what it's doing to our children's brains.

The model **Kim Kardashian** is an inveterate user of social media, and her anxieties give a flavour of the world children are trying to negotiate today:

I'm such a perfectionist that I'm not really completely happy with my body. I don't like my thighs, I wear Spanx a lot, they're like the greatest invention. I like to do a little QuickTrim cleanse before bikini time and photo shoots and if I've got something coming up I don't eat as bad and I work out all the time.

The TV presenter **Davina McCall** provides a much-needed corrective:

We owe it to society to all be more truthful about ourselves and our lives, and actually, I really understand how hard it is to say sometimes 'I'm not perfect and everything is not going great and I have a tough life' but actually, when I do do that, or I say 'This is my 73rd selfie because I hated the other 72', people respond so well to it because actually, what any of us show on any kind of social media is a complete lie!

We're showing the very, very best of our lives, and we need to let young people know that, because otherwise we are breeding an entire generation of perfectionists and none of us can achieve perfection. We're all works in progress.

AGE 17
There's no such word as can't

The cool kids at college were spending every weekend at parties, drinking beer and partnering up. I wasn't invited. I was part of a smaller, less exclusive, group of geeks, who rode about on our bikes. Seventeen-year-old boys riding bicycles back then was like not having a mobile now – slightly more than odd.

We weren't where the cool boys and girls were and certainly nowhere near any music or beer, but we were outside and tried to make the best of the situation. Cycling came with strings attached for me, though.

Dad was a member of the local cycling club. He had all the gear and looked like a Tour de France rider. Every Sunday morning, he would disappear with his club mates, only returning, hungry and happy, just in time for lunch. Never a sign of an accident or a problem with his bike.

By contrast, I came to feel that I should never have taken the stabilizers off my bike. Once, I injured myself when, head down, racing a friend, I rode straight into the back of a parked car. Another time, I got beaten up by a car driver after I raced him through some lights, and then there was the time I nearly lost a leg when I fell off and the brake lever went straight into my thigh. Three cycle rides resulting in three appearances in hospital.

On one ride, I went the furthest I'd ever been, about sixty miles, all the way to the coast. While I was cycling back, a cable snapped and I was stuck in the top gear. It was really hard and slow work getting up the hills, so I stopped and rang Mum and Dad to see if they could help me.

Mum answered. 'I'll put your dinner in the oven.'

'There's no such word as "can't",' she added.

I genuinely believed my mum when she told us that. Probably because she said it to us almost every day of our childhood. It was instilled in me. I was obviously born to be able to do anything.

There were many times when I doubted it – doubted I could do my homework well enough, get picked for the school football team, get to the shops and back in time for my favourite TV programme, get a Saturday job, make a cake, get to Grandma's after school ... or cycle home from the coast.

But I always did because ... there was 'no such word as "can't"'.

That was only one of five key life lessons Mum raised us on:

1. There's no such word as 'can't'.
2. You can only do your best.
3. No one said life was fair.
4. If you don't ask, you don't get.
5. Don't take no for an answer.

It might explain why, after discovering that creating game ideas wasn't actually on the curriculum at art college and I was being judged more on my (lack of) ability to paint and draw, I found myself in front of the careers officer with my dad, explaining, quite naturally, that, as I now knew I wasn't good enough to be a professional footballer and it was looking unlikely that I was going to make it as a games inventor, I now wanted to be an F1 motor racing driver, the rationale being that I loved spending Sunday afternoons listening to F1 on the radio.

And there's 'no such word as "can't"'.

Which, as it turned out, was actually quite a hard mantra to live up to.

Cause: unrealistic expectations (real or perceived)

School, advertising and social media impose almost impossibly high expectations on teenagers, but, without knowingly doing so, parents and other important adults can amplify that.

We are all aware of the pushy parent (the 'tiger mum'), often foisting their own ambitions on their child. 'Come on, you can do it better than that' is the oft-heard refrain. The child ends up needing to achieve more to feel they deserve their place on the pedestal they have been raised up onto than for their own happiness.

But the feeling of both inadequacy and perfectionism can also form from a child seeing important adults achieve things they believe they will never be able to themselves. For an adult, cycling fifty miles takes training, typing at a hundred words a minute takes practice, and making an amazing cake every time happens through trial and error.

But, generally, we share only the finished product with children, not the learning and practice that have gone into it. It can be viewed as a sign of weakness to discuss what you have put into achieving something but while we hide this, young children are growing up believing they'll never be able to do these things.

Adults should inspire children by letting them know how they, and everyone else, practises, trains, tries, fails and fails again, before they achieve anything. Tell them that. Ignore societal pressure to be strong and not vulnerable in front of children. Otherwise, they will grow up believing, like many of us, that they need to hide this half of their lives, afraid others will think they are a failure if they achieve less than what they believe their work should amount up to.

Boys, especially, find it almost impossible to discuss or display any sign of weakness. Cutting and other forms of self-harm are becoming an epidemic among girls as a visible way of communicating their anxiety about not feeling good enough.[1] Boys, by contrast, do not communicate so much, even in this deeply negative way, and consequently we are now seeing the tragedy of an increasing number of suicides among teenagers and young students, particularly boys.[2]

---

1 NHS England figures show that the number of girls treated as hospital inpatients after cutting themselves quadrupled between 2005 and 2015, while the number of boys admitted had more than doubled.

2 The Centre for Suicide Research and Prevention, at Hong Kong University, found that the number of suicides of full-time students in England and Wales increased from 75 in 2007 to 134 in 2015. Britain's student suicide rate rose from 6.6 per 100,000 students to 10.3 between 2007 and 2016.

No one should grow up believing they are not good enough.

We have to break the cycle.

Advertising and neoliberal values lead adults to raise the next generation to be better versions of themselves. But not everything needs to always be better, richer and more successful.

Least of all we humans.

The following is an extract from the article 'The Dangerous Downsides of Perfectionism' at bbc.com, by Amanda Ruggeri, special projects editor and senior journalist.

A recent meta-analysis, the most complete on the suicide – perfectionism link to date, found that nearly every perfectionistic tendency – including being concerned over mistakes, feeling like you are never good enough, having critical parents, or simply having high personal standards – was correlated with thinking about suicide more frequently. (The two exceptions: being organised or demanding of others).

Some of those criteria, particularly pressure from parents and perfectionistic concerns, also were correlated with more suicide attempts.

'All or nothing' thinking can lead perfectionists to interpret failures as catastrophes that, in extreme circumstances, are seen as warranting death,' the researchers wrote. 'Our findings also join a wider literature suggesting that when people experience their social world as pressure-filled, judgmental, and hypercritical, they think about and/or engage in various potential means of escape (e.g. alcohol misuse and binge eating), including suicide.

Ellie Soutter

Ellie Soutter was one of the most progressive junior female snowboard athletes of Great Britain. She became vice champion of the world in the Junior Freeride World Tour, winner of a bronze medal for Team GB at the European Youth Olympics and was tipped to be one of GB's strongest contenders for the next Winter Olympics.

Ellie died by suicide on her eighteenth birthday.

The following is an extract about Ellie Soutter from an article by Amie Henderson for *Source Magazine*:

On the face of it, Ellie had it all. Born in the UK and living in the Alps since the age of nine, with her doting dad Tony, Ellie had become one of the most promising athletes on Team GB's British Snowboard squad. Back in the UK, Ellie's mum Lorraine was her biggest cheerleader; she had the support and encouragement of her entire family.

When Ellie took her own life on her 18th birthday it rocked our community to its very core. We live alongside each other without realising that, for some, life is not OK. For some, life is filled with too much pressure, too much expectation, too much worry. But surely not for Ellie? Adoring parents, so many close friends and her dream career as a professional snowboarder right there in front of her. How could this happen?

'Young athletes are under an incredible amount of pressure,' Ellie's dad tells me. 'When their friends are all going out, doing the things that normal teenagers do, athletes have to think carefully about the consequences of a night out. This can be hard for teenagers; they feel like they're missing out on so much.'

Education was also a big issue. To cram the final years of her education in around snowboarding, Ellie was home schooled. 'This could be lonely for her and it reduced her social life massively,' says Tony. 'Ellie would call me before every single competition,' Lorraine tells me. 'I'd calm her down and tell her the outcome didn't really matter. She worried about her performance all the time.' Ellie gave no clue to her personal struggles. Not to her Team GB teammates, her coaches or her closest friends. 'She didn't want people to know she had issues,' Lorraine tells me. 'She was the life and soul of the party and she had a wicked sense of humour. You'd never know the loneliness she suffered. She felt it just wasn't cool to show any signs of weakness.'

continued ...

'Ellie just wanted to be the best at everything and not let anybody down. Unfortunately she missed a flight for training with the GB squad. She felt she'd let them down, felt she'd let me down and tragically it just takes one silly little thing like that to tip someone over the edge, because there's a lot of pressure on children.'

A picture emerges of a stressed teenager. One who felt every gram of expectation on her young shoulders. I never saw Ellie looking unhappy. Her Instagram feed is filled with fun. Her Facebook bio reads 'Occasionally doing cool things with my snowboard'. Ellie gave no clue to her private struggles. She was humble and grateful and had a smile for everyone she met.

'She had no clue of how many people admired her talent. If I even dared post a podium picture or suggest how proud I was of Ellie's achievements, she shot me down straight away,' Tony tells me. 'We were so proud of her, but she didn't want the limelight. She just wanted to stand out for her abilities on her snowboard. That was Ellie.'

'Of course, I was super proud of her snowboarding achievements,' Ellie's mum Lorraine tells me, 'but I was already so proud of her. Young people need to know that it's OK to speak up. 'This is Ellie's legacy; it's OK not to be OK. It's OK to ask for help.'

Ellie's family have since established the Ellie Soutter Foundation. Its aim is to help other young winter sports athletes to fund their training and give them the essential skills to deal with the unavoidable stress, pressure and expectation that comes with competing at the highest level.

AGE 18
Collaborate and compromise
Achieving success without perfection (1)

Only two weeks after my eighteenth birthday I received a letter informing me that I would have to do jury service.

My immediate reaction was relief. It meant I could escape for a while from showing my art college tutors my embarrassingly poor attempts at drawing. But what it actually meant was that I ended up, a geeky eighteen-year-old kid, sitting in a jury room with eleven proper grown-ups, having just listened to three days of posh yachtsmen telling us that, for a while, they had thought their friend was 'stealing harbour marinas', after seeing an article suggesting just that, alongside a grainy picture of him, in the *Yachtsman* magazine. The friend was claiming money from the magazine for damage to his reputation. And the crazy upshot was, if we thought the magazine was guilty, we had to decide how much money to award him. It could be any amount. One million pounds? I knew nothing.

The magazine had apologized for using his photo and tried to justify it by arguing that you couldn't really see it was him and that, in any case, it was obviously an April Fools piece for their April edition. No one steals marinas, after all. That's not what the yachtsman's friends wanted us to believe.

We couldn't agree what decision to make. There was a lot of dead-end conversation and jurors staring at the floor, not even knowing where to start. It was looking like it was going to take a while. Eventually we got to a situation where half the jury thought the magazine was guilty and the other half thought that it was obviously a joke.

It would almost have been more enjoyable to be back at college.

The magazine was probably guilty really, but how much money should we award if we made that decision? I had an idea. Me. The kid who was useless at school.

'Why don't we make the magazine guilty but award the yachtsman nothing, no money at all? They are technically guilty but it was obviously a joke.'

All eleven adults instantly liked that, although perhaps they just liked the fact it would be an unexpected decision rather than the right one. We were back in court in front of the judge, yachtsman and representatives of the magazine within five minutes.

Our foreman announced that we had decided that the magazine was guilty.

Cue cheers from the yachtsman's team.

'How much do you award as damages?' asked the judge.

'Can we award nothing?' replied the foreman.

'Er, you have to award something. At least the lowest coin of the realm,' instructed the judge.

'Half a pence damages to the yachtsman.'

Cue cheers from the magazine's team.

The following day Dad brought the newspaper home. 'You're in the *Daily Telegraph*!' he announced loudly.

My idea, our decision, was reported in the newspaper. I liked that. It made me feel good. Apart from inventing some games, it was the first thing I had ever done that had impressed anybody.

Learning: collaborate and compromise

We are raised to be competitive, not collaborative. We are taught to hide our schoolwork from others and to beat them in tests. No wonder collaborating when we reach adulthood is low on our list of priorities.

Perfectionists also struggle to compromise, as they possess the uncompromising belief that things are either right or wrong. There is no middle ground for perfectionists. They believe they can trust only their own, fully comprehensive decision-making process. So, they struggle alone for hour upon hour, day upon day, week upon week, year upon year even.

But success can be achieved more easily, more quickly and far more enjoyably through collaboration and compromise.

Any success I have had has only come after I have worked on other people's ideas I didn't think were as good as my own, kept quiet when I disagreed with others, or collaborated instead of competed with competitors.

And, of course, compromise has been the only way I have played my part in bringing a positive conclusion to any argument or disagreement I've had at work or home. That said, I have also wasted hours, days, weeks and, indeed, years of my life and lost friendships trying the opposite route.

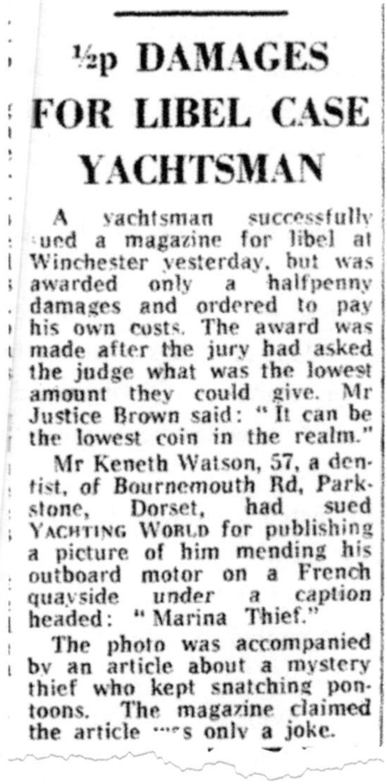

½p DAMAGES FOR LIBEL CASE YACHTSMAN

A yachtsman successfully sued a magazine for libel at Winchester yesterday, but was awarded only a halfpenny damages and ordered to pay his own costs. The award was made after the jury had asked the judge what was the lowest amount they could give. Mr Justice Brown said: "It can be the lowest coin in the realm."

Mr Keneth Watson, 57, a dentist, of Bournemouth Rd, Parkstone, Dorset, had sued YACHTING WORLD for publishing a picture of him mending his outboard motor on a French quayside under a caption headed: "Marina Thief."

The photo was accompanied by an article about a mystery thief who kept snatching pontoons. The magazine claimed the article was only a joke.

Article on the jury decision in the *Daily Telegraph*

AGE 19
A not 'good enough' teenager

It had been interesting to do the jury service and exciting to be in the newspaper. I'd had a glimpse of a world that I wanted to play a role in – one where people listened to me, took me seriously and thought that what I was doing was actually all right.

So being back in a world where none of that was the case was a real downer. My sister Sue had left home and she was two years younger than me. I felt like I was living in the suburbs of my own life. I was in a rut and I was losing weight. Too much weight.

It had all started with Dad standing in my bedroom on the verge of being angry. He was asking if the letter that he and Mum had just received from the art college saying I'd left a month earlier was referring to me or whether it was just a mix-up.

It wasn't.

'What the hell have you been doing for the last month then?' Now he was actually angry.

Art college had started well, but when the teachers discovered I could create only ideas and not drawings, paintings or sculptures, I could tell that they had lost faith in me and so I followed their lead and did the same. For the last month I'd been leaving home at the normal time and just hanging around all day.

I hated college, but I hated wasting my life more.

Now Mum and Dad knew.

'You need to find yourself a job. Now.'

'On my bike?' I was tempted to retort, though I was too scared to do so.

'It costs us to have you living here, you know!'

And that is how I went from dreams of doing something creative or even driving an F1 car to becoming a local shop assistant.

Dad was happy, though. I could pay my 'keep' now. I wouldn't cost him by living at home anymore.

I wasn't happy.

For me, a geeky, spotty, teenage boy, it meant leaving the sanctuary of my bedroom on a daily basis and facing twenty-five girls of my age and twenty-five older, scary (to me), women on the shop floor. It forced me to have to think more about what I looked like. Not because I wanted to look good; I just didn't want to stand out for looking bad. It was pressure I could have done without. My bedroom didn't care if I had spots or ate too much chocolate.

So, I had my hair permed.

What?!

That's not what nineteen-year-old boys in an army town did. The idea was to look like Kevin Keegan, the current captain of the England football team, or the singer David Bowie. It was done by Mum's friend in our kitchen. It looked OK.

Or at least I thought it did.

Some people were a bit taken aback. The ones who still recognized me, that is.

It served its purpose, though. I did feel OK about myself and for a while I quite enjoyed working in the shop. They had a music department, selling CDs, and I put everything into making it the best music department in the whole town.

I even went out with one of the Saturday girls. Briefly.

But, still, behind my closed bedroom door was the only place I could be free to be myself and relax. I was getting more into music, particularly a singer called Gary Numan. He seemed like me – awkward with other people and not like everyone else.

His was a reassuring voice in my head, telling me that being like me was OK. It could be cool to be a little 'distant' from other people:

I spent my wages on more magazines. They gave a glimpse of the life that was possible, not for me, but for people who were lucky enough

Me, with that perm, that I can now laugh at

to be good-looking, talented and rich. I was no longer losing myself in fantasy worlds but in a real world, just one that was unobtainable to me. If my magazines were anything to go by, it seemed that everyone in the pop world always looked great, were happy, went to parties, wore cool clothes, went on dates and got drunk. Everyone except Gary Numan.

I loved the world I lived in through the pages of the magazines in my bedroom. Magazines were almost my best friends. They shared the life I really wanted to live, the life that would get me friends and make me happy and successful. The other side of the coin was that I didn't want to live the life at the shop anymore – alongside fifty women I didn't have much, if anything, in common with. Apart from permed hair.

I didn't fit.

Losing weight started out as a way to fit in. I hoped that it would make me less spotty and stand out less. It wasn't about meeting a new girl, though. When, every lunchtime, all the sales assistants would congregate in the canteen, I'd disappear to the newsagents to read the pop magazines or to the local arcade to try to beat my highest score on the gaming machines. I made a commitment to myself to eat less, though. And I couldn't fail at that. Losing weight became more about not breaking that commitment than looking better.

There was a hurdle: I had a sweet tooth. Trying to eat less with a sweet tooth takes complete commitment. I would have to go whole days on just one iced bun.

The weight dropped off and didn't stop dropping off. I became obsessed with trying to have no spots, a flat stomach and keeping to my commitment. I lost so much weight that my face and hands started turning purple with cold, and several times I was admitted to hospital because I felt 'a bit weird in my head'.

The doctors couldn't work out what was causing it. I didn't tell anyone that I hardly ate anything. How could I? I was a bloke.

Eventually, I did at least admit to Mum that I was unhappy. That was the closest I could get to admitting I was trapped in a spiral of hating my life and consequently not eating.

'Do something about it then,' she said. 'There's no such word as "can't".'

Cause: advertising

Impressionable children are targeted, day after day, by millions of perfect images and messages from highly funded advertisers, employing the very best people and software. Every single advert aims to make them believe they are not good enough and will only be less spotty, thinner, cooler, faster, healthier … more successful, once they buy their product.

It would be a miracle if they didn't succumb. And by 'succumbing' I mean losing their self-confidence and believing that they will only feel happy and successful if they buy their spot cream, low-fat snack, expensive clothes or branded trainers.

This messaging especially impacts teenagers when it is consumed alongside content they trust and in what they think of as the 'safe' confines of their bedroom. Their guard is down and they are more easily manipulated. YouTubers and Instagram stars with their product endorsements and advertorials do the work of the advertisers only too successfully.

Children should be taught more about the mechanics of branding and advertising. But until that happens, look at what they scroll through and note the adverts they are consuming – the adverts that are gradually eroding their self-confidence. Try instigating an honest conversation about these ads and how they make your child feel.

Cordelia Sigurdsson is a student at Cambridge University and here she talks about her perfectionism and struggle with anorexia:

I display all the symptoms: I despise losing to the point I refuse to play board games, the thought of failing my A levels made me feel physically sick and knowing I should have done something I didn't will keep me awake and thinking at night. I am a self-confessed perfectionist.

I don't think you can be a perfectionist and not also be scared to fail: the two come hand in hand – if you fail, surely you are no longer 'perfect'.

When I was a child I would always begin a new sheet of paper if I had to cross out one word on the previous sheet – because the first just didn't look neat enough. If I'm not the best at something, I would much rather give up than have to suffer carrying on at a below average level.

I revised for my A levels for weeks upon weeks because I couldn't bear not to be the best. I refuse to play board games anymore because in all honesty I'm not especially good at them, and I just can't bear to lose. If I'm not the best at something, I automatically dislike it. This isn't me being big headed, rather it is the nature of the perfectionist who seeks obsessively to triumph in whatever they do.

These examples are soul destroying for a perfectionist because it means suddenly that you are not the best at something: someone else, somewhere, has figured it out – so why can't I?

This little voice in your head may be pushy and unforgivingly motivational but, equally, it will eat you from the inside out when something goes wrong, whenever you fail or think that you might. In fact, the risk of failure is entirely overestimated; but still we see its possibility in every endeavour we pursue.

I suffered with anorexia, an illness that I am entirely convinced was linked to perfectionism and my consequent fear of failure. I was absolutely petrified of failing my GCSEs, of choosing a sixth form, of losing friends, and of growing up and not being successful. Food became the only thing I felt I could really control. I was referred as a hospital outpatient where, as they questioned me on my personality, eating habits and health, they asked:

'Would you describe yourself as a perfectionist?' I remember nodding solemnly, and they returned, 'Ah, of course, they all are, bet you hate losing as well.'

The overwhelming fear of failure and the fragility of the perfect persona is forever present and sometimes it is so overwhelming that it physically hurts. For me, this was through food, for others it can emerge in a whole host of different ways.

I have, since this time, learnt how to fight against these feelings, started to figure out how to fail and how not to punish myself for it. In other words, my eating disorder recovery was not just about gaining weight and being healthy again – it was about learning that failure is a part of life and perfection is a goal that nobody will reach.

Not being good at one thing, even a silly children's board game, does not mean that you should punish, or respect yourself any less.

Symptom: food issues

Research shows perfectionists are more likely to suffer from anorexia.[3] The obsessive striving for thinness is a manifestation of their obsession with aiming for unattainably high standards, applied to their own bodies.

It can often be the first sign of perfectionism in teenagers – their body is the one thing they can still try to have control over, when everything around them appears to be out of their control and much of it causing stress and anxiety.

Overachievement at school has also been observed among anorexics, as a result of their perfectionist behaviour. A Swedish study found that hospitalization for eating disorders was around twice as common among girls who achieved high grades.

For years what I was eating preoccupied my thoughts more often than anything else. I still believed that, if I put weight on, I would have failed – failed to maintain my own high standards.

As parents, my wife and I have had to deal with food disorders within our family. At no point did any doctor ever mention perfectionism or mental wellbeing generally. It was literally about calories. If you find yourself in the same situation, make sure that you see a mental health expert and get to the real reason for your child's apparent lack of appetite.

3 Samantha Lloyd, Jenny Yiend, Ulrike Schmidt and Kate Tchanturia, 'Perfectionism in Anorexia Nervosa: Novel Performance Based Evidence', *PLoS ONE* 9(10) (October 2014).

:(Part Two :)

Chasing perfection

AGE 20
Perfectionist adult

I did what I was told. I did do something about it.

I got my mum's typewriter and typed out forty-five letters, using the two fingers that could work out where the keys were. I locked myself in my bedroom, didn't watch any TV or go out, until I was finished. I kept making mistakes. It took four days – one personalized letter to each BBC radio station in Britain. I now wanted to be a DJ.

There's no such word as 'can't'.

Music was the subject I knew more about than anything else, more than anyone else I knew. I'd spent the last three years selling records in the shop and spending all my wages on the latest releases and pop magazines. I just had to find a name and an address for every radio station, post the letter and cross my fingers.

My music provided the perfect (and loud) soundtrack for the four-day execution of the plan to escape my own life:

Same old boring Sunday morning
Old man's out washing the car
Mum's in the kitchen cooking Sunday dinner
Her best meal, moaning while it lasts
Johnny's upstairs in his bedroom sitting in the dark
Annoying the neighbours with his punk rock electric guitar

This is the sound
This is the sound of the suburbs ...

It summed up how I felt and motivated me to keep going. I needed to escape the life I was living, getting thinner and spending more time in hospital. Escape a life that was nowhere near the perfect life I now (without realizing) needed it to be.

Three weeks later I had received just eight replies. And they were all identical: 'BBC jobs are appointed centrally, from London.'

So, I wrote one more letter.

And received one reply.

It offered me the glimmer of a chance. An interview for a three-month contract, not as an actual DJ, broadcasting to millions, but as a librarian, in the biggest music library in the world – getting out and putting back again, in their rightful alphabetical place, the music that would be broadcast to millions.

It might not have been for a job as a DJ but it was still music; it was still the BBC. I was very enthusiastic ... obsessed more like. I wanted this job. I needed this job.

I got it!

At last, this was a real chance to prove to everyone that they were wrong about me – my teachers, the football team 'managers', the other boys and girls, my mum and dad, the girl at the disco, my manager at the shop. *Everyone.*

I wasn't lazy. I wasn't useless. I'll show them I'm not a failure.

I had to leave my little evening job as a volunteer DJ on the local hospital radio station. We had a photocopied magazine distributed to our quite ill, therefore very captive, audience. It had a profile on each of the DJs. On mine was the answer to the question 'What is your ambition?': 'To be the best at whatever I do.' I meant it.

I was joining the BBC. I couldn't believe it. Getting the job, though, meant, once again, that I had to leave the sanctuary of my bedroom, and this time, potentially, for ever.

On the first day I had butterflies in my stomach. I went downstairs to breakfast, cycled from home to the station, took the train to London and then walked over the Thames and through Soho to BBC Broadcasting House.

It was the longest journey of my life.

Only thirty-five miles by train, but in my head a million, to a world I had only seen in my magazines. By the time I walked into the record library I was scared stiff. I was just a kid from suburbia who only knew about music. I was met by people who had been to university, flown abroad for holidays, read serious newspapers, drank Beaujolais Nouveau and went to the theatre.

I had flunked school, stayed in a caravan for holidays, read comics, drank lager and black, and watched sci-fi movies.

Music was the only thing I could talk equally to the others about, where my knowledge held up, without fear of embarrassing myself, without fear of people finding me out. So, that's all I spoke about – with lots of enthusiasm.

Like hiding behind my permed hair, hiding behind my obsessive musical knowledge seemed to work: after a few months, three of the others asked if I wanted to share a flat in London with them. Amazing.

As I finally left home, I asked Mum whether the bedroom would always be mine. She said yes, but I still took most of its contents with me. Up on the walls of my bedroom in our new flat went my posters of Captain Kirk and Gary Numan. But none of my new flatmates had posters; they had prints. I had my magazines but they had books.

The real me was out of his depth here.

I'd just left the shop, where I'd served old ladies, to join the BBC, where I was serving famous DJs. I went red with embarrassment whenever anyone I recognized walked past – which was most people – because these were my heroes, from the pages of my magazines, to whom I had listened on the radio under my bedcovers.

I was starting with the lowest job, but I quickly became the fastest on the team at completing tasks. It was the best way to stop anyone finding out that I didn't know about anything other than music.

People seemed to like someone who did their job very well. They were nice to me. I thought they were just being kind, but they actually seemed to take me seriously. How ridiculous was that? They didn't appear to be looking down at me. They appeared to enjoy our conversations as much as I did. As long as they were about music.

The Debbie Harry and Princess Leia posters came down, and my confidence went up.

... And so, too, did my weight. In all the nervousness and busyness of getting the job and leaving home I justified to myself that I could, just this once, break a commitment to myself. I allowed myself to eat properly again. I had a new commitment now ...

Cause: the myth of perfectionism

Daily, children and teenagers feel stressed at having to perform at their best, to fulfil other people's expectations of them – parents raising them to be better versions of themselves, teachers expecting them to reach the highest attainment in every subject, and advertisers, online 'friends' and heroes/role models imposing impossibly perfect ideals for them to live up to.

They feel they are not good enough for that.

Because no one is good enough for that.

But many now believe they can convince themselves, and everyone else, they are good enough, if they make certain things they think, say and do absolutely perfect. If they can make aspects (not everything) of their work, their body, their friendships, their family, perfect, then they can finally 'achieve' the happiness they remember unconditionally feeling as a small child.

So, what do they do? They dedicate their adult life to trying to prove themselves to all the people they share their lives with, all day, every day, at the expense of their actual relationships with them.

They become perfectionists ...

This myth of what achieving perfection promises is behind the epidemic we now have of mental-health issues – from relationship breakdowns, workaholism, anxiety and depression to burnout, loneliness and self-harm.

Symptom: imposter syndrome

Very much in hindsight, I now understand that I wasn't becoming more confident; instead I had developed a mask – that of the infallible music expert – to hide the real, boring, geeky me and to present a person that people might think was good, that they might like. I couldn't let anyone see the real me now. I had subconsciously left the imperfect me in suburbia.

This mask of perfectionism is often called 'imposter syndrome', as the sufferer knows others can't see the real them but they worry that, one day, someone will and that their life will start to fall apart.

People are suffering anxiety simply because we have been taught to not let anyone else see our self-doubt. It's why I made sure I hid my real self. To others, I was confident and knowledgeable about music. In reality, inside, I was a maelstrom of stress and loneliness as I waved goodbye to inward, emotional happiness and looked for outward, emotionless perfection.

AGE 21
Have to put it right

It was the 13 July. Twelve noon in London, 7 a.m. in Philadelphia and around the world it was time for Live Aid.

Live Aid was the music event of the last century, a follow-up to the best-selling charity single 'Do They Know It's Christmas?', both were put together by the dishevelled singer of the Irish band the Boomtown Rats, inspired by a BBC news report about the famine in Ethiopia by the BBC reporter Michael Buerk:

> Dawn, and as the sun breaks through the piercing chill of night on the plain outside Korem. It lights up a biblical famine. Now! In the 20th century. This place, say workers here, is the closest thing to hell on earth.

The report was incredibly distressing but it was watched by millions. Despite being a rock star, with no background in politics or humanitarian aid, Bob Geldof decided to do something about it. He gathered together as many of the world's pop stars as he could, released the Band Aid single and then put on the Live Aid concert, all to raise funds. Nothing had ever happened like this before.

Almost every major star or band played live: David Bowie, George Michael, Elton John, U2, Madonna and Queen. Over 1 billion people watched globally. It felt like literally the whole world was talking about the amazing bands and their performances. They were brilliant but I had been affected far more by a video created for probably the least well-known act on the bill, the American rock band the Cars.

The news report footage, showing tens of thousands of Ethiopian men, women and children, dying of cold and starvation, was used as the video for the Cars song 'Drive'. It was shown on giant video screens from the stage and on our TV screens around the world:

Who's gonna tell you when
It's too late

Who's gonna tell you things
Aren't so great.

Who's gonna pick you up
When you fall?

Once seen, it was unforgettable. I couldn't show anyone the real me, but this film knew how to get through. It really got me. Right there.

How could this be happening in the world? How could people allow their fellow human beings – men, women and children – to die like this in such huge numbers? How was something so wrong possible? I couldn't comprehend it. I felt a strong compulsion that I needed to do something to help put it right.

I watched Bob Geldof go about making things happen. There were educated politicians in suits meant to be doing their best for everyone but not achieving nearly enough. So 'fuck 'em!' The normal way, the accepted way, wasn't working, and Geldof wasn't going to put up with it.

However big, however apparently complicated a problem appears to be, whoever you are, you can do something. You just follow your heart and do your best. That's the example Bob Geldof was setting. If he could do it, anyone could do it.

Even me?

I didn't tell anyone but I genuinely believed I could get my first passport, hire a truck and drive food to Ethiopia. I made calls. 'Hello, I'm a 21-year-old record librarian …'

Over the next few months, as Live Aid drifted out of the news and out of sight, I had a decision to make. It would never drift out of my mind. Once an injustice was in my head, unless I did something about it, it would remain in there for ever, nagging away, until I actually acted or could rationalize to myself a reason not to act, just so I could avoid living the rest of my life with a guilty conscience.

But the demand I felt to do something was being undermined by my everyday, normal priorities – making sure people always thought I was good at my job and earning enough money to pay my rent being the main ones. So, in the short term, I did rationalize my failure to act. I told myself that I didn't know what the latest situation was, and that no doubt someone, somewhere, was doing something about it.

My understanding of the world was broken, though. There was more to life than looking forward to the next great album release. Even at twenty-one I knew that one day I would have to do something.

Trait: inflexible about values

Perfectionists are often preoccupied and vocal with regards to moral or ethical behaviour. They are over-conscientious and completely inflexible about their high standards and values. Things are either right or wrong. There is no grey area. If something isn't right, it must be wrong.

Perfectionists need to always do the right thing and to avoid any anxiety that they might not be doing that; they investigate every single minor factor to make sure that they are getting it right, every single time – from throwing rubbish in the bin to putting the world to rights.

They constantly question whether their own actions are right. Am I using too much water? Should I be a vegetarian/vegan? Am I raising my children in the way my parents would approve of? Is my marriage as perfect as it should be?

This preoccupation can lead to many vicious arguments, to dead ends, with those they love, simply because they believe something even just slightly different. Perfectionists will argue to the bitter end, rather than be able to consider compromising with a different view. I know I am right; therefore, you must be wrong.

AGE 22
Finding your tribe
Escaping the demand for perfection (2)

After spending weeks working out how I could help in Ethiopia, normal life in the record library started to feel a lot like the normal life I had had before. I could now be the best at putting records on shelves without it stretching me. So, instead I was being stretched in another direction, by the glimpse of fulfilment that could be possible by achieving something that I really *needed* to do, rather than just *wanted* to do.

I'd discovered, by failing spectacularly at trying several times, that I probably wouldn't ever get a promotion at the BBC. They seemed to put qualifications ahead of anything else, and I hadn't got any. So I wasn't getting many interviews for internal jobs. It seemed it would be impossible for me to move up the ladder. There were people who had spent decades around the library's bottom rung. I didn't want to add to their number.

I had been there two years. It could have been a job for life, so it did seem crazy, but I knew, in my post-Live Aid thinking, it was no longer for me.

As soon as I had decided that I had to leave the shop assistant job, I didn't want anything more to do with it and I couldn't wait to get away. The same thing was happening here. Everyone was still friendly to me but I was spending a lot less time with them. At the shop I spent every lunchtime alone in the arcade. This time I was spending every weekend alone, going to watch football matches.

I went to every single West Ham game, home and away. Bobby Moore had retired by then, but I was watching my new heroes, week in, week out. I was travelling and standing alongside thousands of strangers, who all had only this one passion in common. We were every age, every level of aggression (I was obviously at the cowardly end), every haircut, accent, class and trade. We shoved each other on the train, battled to get through the turnstiles and to get a drink at half-time, invaded each other's space and were rude and aggressive to one other.

But when we scored ... wow!

All our differences and tensions disappeared, and we just jumped up and down in happy childlike joy, piled down to the front of the terracing and hugged each other. And for that very short moment we were all best friends, without a care in the world. We were all part of something but that euphoria and sense of community vanished as quickly as it came. By the time we left the ground and headed back to our normal lives we had no further obligation to one another, other than to say hello if we happened to be standing next to the same supporter at the following match.

I was interested in meeting new people; it was when I got to know them that the problems arose – the pressure I put on myself to form the perfect friendship or working relationship; the pressure I put on them to meet my impossibly high standards. My relationship with football and my fellow supporters was an escape from these real-life pressures. I didn't have to get to know them.

For ninety minutes every week I got to experience that same 'third space' freedom I had felt in my childhood bedroom, where I had escaped the constant pressure to have to do everything right for everyone.

Football was the only thing in my life that hadn't changed since those times in my bedroom. It was my anchor. Whether we won, lost, scored or conceded, I needed the escape from real life, in exactly the same way as I did back then as a child.

It was only an escape, though; it didn't solve my problem. I still felt all my decisions had to be perfect. What could I possibly do now that might provide the success and fulfilment I was searching for?

It ended up being West Ham's best ever season. To celebrate, I asked Dad if he would paint a team of Subbuteo toy footballers in all the different kits the team had ever worn.

He did. And, as usual with my father, they were absolutely, bloody, amazingly, *perfect*.

Escaping the demand for perfection (2)

Due to the ongoing pressure they feel, many perfectionists need time with only themselves for company, but at the same they don't want to be lonely. A tribe of likeminded people is the ideal solution. It provides an outlet for them to participate in something they enjoy alongside others who share their interests. They can join in as much or as little as they want. It is a community, but one where the perfectionist can retain control over their own involvement and interactions.

AGE 23
Trying to prove everyone wrong

I was still at the BBC and being well paid. I still couldn't believe I had got there at all. But here I was handing in my resignation and willingly becoming unemployed. How did it get to that?

I had started arranging some small gigs in London for bands from back home. I was really enjoying it, but most importantly I was being taken seriously enough that I thought I could be a full-time band manager – specifically of a band called Jim Jiminee, who I genuinely believed to be brilliant. I wanted to make it happen for them, help them sign a record deal and release a single – that would be amazing.

There's no such word as 'can't', remember.

There was no money in managing bands, though. I wasn't even sure exactly what the job entailed. Try to make a band famous, essentially?

This was no job for life, but it was something I really believed in. That's what was important to me. Do something properly or don't do it at all. This was my next 'all' to put my every single waking hour, my every single waking thought into.

I could just about afford to risk it because money wasn't important to me and, luckily, there was a financial safety net – government enterprise schemes. They would pay my rent in full, plus give me a small weekly amount to live on, as long as I started my own business.

So I created 'Third Angle Projection' band management. My very own little business. The name was inspired by some work I remembered Dad doing in his job – a drawing that showed the whole of a product from three different angles.

I was visiting Mum and Dad less often by now, and as neither they nor I were very good at ringing each other, I was speaking to them less overall. But I did proudly call Dad to tell him about what I called my first business. But then we had a stupid argument about moving some of the stuff I still had at home, and this led to the phone being put down. After that call, I didn't talk to Mum or Dad again for nearly a year. They thought they were right, so they were waiting for me to call them. I obviously thought I was right, so I was waiting for them to ring me.

Either way, it was going to be a long wait. And even though I had buried my vulnerability, my parents not talking to me was one of the things that could still get through to it. It meant I just couldn't face a difficult five-minute conversation with them, even if it might have resulted in things returning to normal. I hadn't achieved anything yet for them to take me seriously; I was still their underachieving son. I still felt like I was a failure in their eyes.

Rather than call them, I needed to prove them wrong. I needed to become successful so they would be proud of me. That would give them a reason to call me.

In my dreams, the band would get a record contract, release a single, and Mum and Dad would hear it on the radio. They would literally hear my success for themselves.

However much I worked and declined any invitation to take time off for a night out, it wasn't going to happen overnight. So, we didn't speak – at least not until nine months later, when I knocked on their door on Christmas morning and they put my presents under the tree, just like every other Christmas morning in my childhood.

The new year was starting with little family support, no girlfriend and no workmates, but I had a band I believed in and the goal to achieve – to prove everyone wrong. That's all I needed.

Symptom: workaholism

Perfectionist workers have a relentless drive to become successful because everything they believe points to the fact that this will finally and conclusively prove they are good enough. They often literally cannot commit to anyone or anything else until they have achieved something. Achievement is everything, an obsession. Anything else, everyone else, becomes a distraction.

Most prefer to work alone. Relationships aren't needed. Money isn't needed. Looking after their own welfare isn't even needed.

That's why they can give up a job for life. They value even themselves lower than their output. They take little enjoyment in work. It is about what they achieve, not the process.

Perfectionists believe they will only be happy when others believe they are not a failure. Until that time, the less they have to interact with them, the better.

Sir Tom Hunter, Scotland's first billionaire and largest philanthropist, put it thus: 'The thing that people don't understand about most entrepreneurs is that we are driven by self-doubt. A lot of successful people outwardly you think are so confident but we're all trying to prove ourselves. All the time.'

AGE 24
Nothing will prove *everyone* wrong

The office of Third Angle Projection Band Management was literally an old-fashioned dressing table, in the corner of a small bedroom, in a badly furnished shared London flat. Since leaving my original flat share, it also doubled up as my new home.

Having a nice office was irrelevant, though; I was on the phone nonstop, booking the band as many gigs as possible, culminating in the most important one to which I badgered as many record company personnel as possible to come and see if they wanted to sign the band to a record contract. Just one did, but it was a good one: MCA was a global record label with some of the biggest acts in the world. And they were interested! We had an exciting first meeting with them, discussing producers and budgets. And then, a week later, they weren't interested. I just got a message to say sorry, but the deal's off, without any reason given or the promise of a meeting to explain.

That was it; it was over. Dreams of success and proving I could do it faded and died before they had even got off the ground.

Two hours after hearing the news, by the end of the fourth pint, we had an answer: work harder, write better songs, get more gigs and more reviews, and prove them wrong. We could still do it.

Over the rest of the year, I did everything I could to make that happen. I secured reviews and booked the band over eighty gigs. One was with their old university friends Harriet and Dave supporting, in their first performance. They didn't have a name, so we called them the Greengables for the flyer. They were good.

There was lots of work but little money. For the gigs we had a rusty old van and slept on students' floors or drove back through the night, but I loved it. I didn't want for anything, or anyone else in my life, as long as there was progress. We worked harder and longer than anyone else until finally, finally … the phone rang.

A small independent record label wanted to sign the band. It was run by a good bloke, into good music. It felt right. Progress.

More gigs, more live reviews and hour upon hour in the recording studio and eventually, eventually, 'Do It on Thursday', the debut single by Jim Jiminee, managed by Chris Ward, was released.

It was a dream come true. I was managing a band with a single out, and it got played on the radio, from the very building I'd left to try and make that happen, eighteen months earlier.

The homemade, single-take video was shown on TV, and the track made it to number 6 in the independent music chart. This was more than I had even dreamed of achieving.

But, for some reason, not enough people were buying it for it to get into the Top 40 charts. I really thought that records that had all that radio play and their video on TV pretty much automatically got into the charts.

I had achieved my dream but found the edges of my circle of ambition had got bigger. The Independent Chart wasn't enough now.

I needed it to be in the Top 40, otherwise the people I was trying to impress would think we had failed. I needed people to hear it without me having to ring them to tell them every time it was on the radio. My father had certainly never heard of the 'indie music chart'.

I'd done my best, but what was meant to happen didn't. It must have been because of me, something I hadn't done. It was all I could think about: what could I have done differently? Was it my fault? Had I let the band down?

Blaming myself for not achieving what I thought we should, overshadowed what should have been the unbelievable experience of achieving my dream.

I held on tightly to a small glimmer of hope: strangely the single was doing better in Germany than in the UK.

Meanwhile, after their first gig with us, Harriet and Dave changed their name to the Sundays and signed a big record deal in a blaze of publicity and adulation. I was happy for them, but mainly it just motivated me to work even harder, at my 'office' dressing table. I could see my goal, right in front of me.

Cause: the ever-receding ideal of success

Nothing is ever good enough for a perfectionist because, contrary to everything they believe, achievement doesn't achieve what they need it to – a permanent escape from their preoccupation with failure. Success can at best achieve only a very short-lived feeling of contentment, before the perfectionist needs to get back on the treadmill.

I have worked with a lot of very successful perfectionists, but I don't know one who has achieved happiness through their achievements. They never rest on their laurels. They just carry straight on to the next task, often reasoning that they need to prove this first success wasn't just down to luck.

I was talking about this in a radio interview once. When I left the studio, a woman in reception approached me and said, 'That was spot on. It's exactly like that for my husband. He has achieved so much but he keeps on working and working, because when we visit his parents, despite it being in our Rolls-Royce, his father remains totally unimpressed and will still tell him his wheels need a clean, before he's even said hello.' It was the actress Jenny Seagrove, whose partner is the multi-millionaire theatre impresario and owner of Everton Football Club, Bill Kenwright.

Feeling happy and contented never comes from success.

Lifetimes of obsessional, misguided work and putting off relationships and happiness could be saved if this simple truth was taught to every child.

AGE 25
Paying your way

When I was growing up we made do, just like everyone else we knew. Mum would be typing and cleaning, while Dad would split the weekly food shop between two supermarkets, buying the cheapest items at each to make their weekly wages stretch as far as they could. We were shown how to 'make do' with just two sheets of paper after Dad enquired, 'Who is eating the toilet paper?' Nothing ever went to waste in our house. Not even toilet paper.

Literally only once, though, do I remember wishing we had more money…

I was about eleven, and Mum took me to yet another stranger's house, this time to buy some second-hand football boots. When we got there, it was immediately obvious to me, but not to Mum, that they weren't football boots but very old-fashioned, steel toe-capped, ankle-high rugby boots. Much to the detriment of my dream of becoming a professional footballer, the lady refused to stop talking, so I couldn't get a word in. Mum bought them. I had to wear them.

I was still living the same way now. While most of the people I knew were being promoted up the career ladder, with better pay, I was still claiming benefits from the state so that I could continue managing. Money had never been my driver anyway. I never knew what life with it was even like; that was for other people.

My new flatmate Fiona, was earning more than me by recording horse racing results for a business that charged people, via a premium rate phone line, to hear them. She'd also just got herself a new job as a radio DJ. I wasn't jealous, really. It drove me on; if she could do it, so could I. We were no different.

In the short term, I did financially benefit. When her old job called up to offer her work, I suggested I could do it instead. Some of the horses' names were a nightmare to pronounce but it did mean I earned just enough money to last all seven days each week, and not just the current five. As long as I could just about pay my bills and go out a couple of nights a week, I was fine.

There was an upside of having no money. I didn't have any money problems to clog up my head. No unexpected bills, no fines, no mortgage. I didn't have to take things back because I didn't buy anything. There was nothing to distract me.

I didn't want for much money but I would fight tooth and nail if anyone tried to unfairly take what I did have though. I always took it personally and have probably wasted too much of my life, fighting stupid battles over 'unjustified' charges made by gas and electric companies, landlords and letting agencies.

No one I knew had any money in the music world. But if anyone wanted to borrow a fiver, I just couldn't bring myself to offer. I felt I was a good person but, if I did lend it, I'd worry too much that I wouldn't get it back and my relationship with the friend could be ruined. Once they owed me a fiver, I couldn't get it out of my mind until the repayment had been made.

There was no doubt, that most of the people around me would soon get promotions and be earning a lot more than me. I wondered what I'd think then.

Unless, of course, Jim Jiminee had a hit record. They had just released their album and played their biggest ever gig, supporting Squeeze in front of 4,000 people in London.

Harriet and Dave were there. The Sundays were now number 1 in every chart. I desperately wanted to manage them, but the desperation probably came over when we met to discuss it. So, just like everyone else, I had to watch as they made a perfect job of doing it themselves.

Symptom: frugality

Money is generally only important to perfectionists when it's needed to prove that they are making progress towards achieving their goal. If they do earn some, they immediately become frugal, and so are often branded as 'tight'. They don't want to spend any of it and leave themselves vulnerable to the feeling of being worthless.

Some very successful perfectionists believe that having anything less than hundreds of thousands of pounds in the bank is still too close for comfort. Even though they have enough money to last the rest of their lives, they haven't escaped the fear of failure.

Money is saved to guard against any future, unexpected problems. And perfectionists are good at rationalizing anything as a problem. They are savers and not spenders.

Being 'all or nothing' about most things and not wanting to touch the money they have, money matters often fall into the 'nothing' pot – meaning they have no interest in it, apart from not spending it. Therefore, they can often be bad at paying bills, not wanting to deal with a worthless distraction like money.

I know several successful perfectionists who've had the bailiffs knock on their door, simply because they just can't prioritise filing their tax returns or paying their bills.

Many perfectionists are also reluctant to share any of their financial information – how much they earn or how much they paid for something. They are worried that people will judge how good they are by how good they are in handling their money matters: 'Did you really pay that much for that? Seems a lot'; 'Is that all you are paid? Doesn't seem enough for your talents.'

AGE 26
An obsession

It had been three years of working 24/7 trying to get Jim Jiminee into the charts. Three years of dedicating my entire life to it. Sometimes it seemed progress was made only in very tiny steps. There was just enough, though, for me to continue to believe I could still help them achieve it.

We put everything we could into releasing one last single from the album. It was the track everyone liked. We made a brilliant video. I worked away in the flat and set up the biggest tour I could, and managed to get the video shown on TV again. We did everything we could. I did everything I could. Still the record didn't sell enough to make the charts.

The band told me they were going to split up.

I honestly don't remember exactly how this made me feel because I never shared self-doubts with anybody, least of all myself.

I needed to have control over my own life. The previous times when I didn't, I just ran off and escaped from a situation I couldn't face. This was out of my control, I didn't know what to do, how to deal with it. The decision to stop managing a band had been taken out of my hands. I struggled to cope with it.

Had I let the band down? I felt I had. No feeling was guaranteed to get me as down as this one, letting other people down, not living up to their expectations.

I needed to do something quickly, before this depressing feeling completely swamped me. I couldn't dwell. I needed to make something new happen or I needed to disappear from sight again. I couldn't cope with being trapped between flux and uncertainty. Achieving anything was impossible from here.

The best way to escape it? Keep a stiff upper lip, block it out. Don't think about it and start working on something else, asap. That's what I'd been taught.

Living and working out of my bedroom, having no office to go to, no work colleagues, no income, that was all fine because I was a band manager, but now I was just unemployed.

I couldn't stop managing bands though because I was still convinced I could make one successful. It was unfinished business. Only I can decide when I can't achieve something, not someone else.

I needed to manage another band. Now!

Delphi, the backing singer in Jim Jiminee, decided to go solo. I became her manager! Delphi's guitarist also had his own band, Honeychild. That was two bands I was now suddenly managing.

Meanwhile, my old flatmate, Fiona, was presenting a breakfast TV show. She was achieving everything she set out to.

I was so close, I could almost touch it.

Symptom: the elusiveness of enough success

Perfectionists believe that, if they work harder and longer than anyone else, they have the most chance of success. Unfortunately, in 99 per cent of cases this is not true. If it was, everyone would do it and everyone would be successful.

In fact, the opposite has been proven. The longer you work on a task, the less likely it is to be successful, you may miss the right timing and will often waste many working hours being unfocused and unproductive.

Success is dependent on many variables that are not controllable by the amount of time spent on them. There are critical ones, such as how good the proposition is, how well it is communicated, whether the time is right and whether you can access the important people. If one of those isn't right, however long and hard the nights worked, success may well not be possible.

AGE 27
Perfectionist friend

The two new bands I was managing were both from West London, so it seemed to make sense to move there. I shared a tiny flat with Pete, an Irish singer-songwriter friend of Delphi's. The problem was, this was the coolest part of London. Ladbroke Grove was not the suburbia I came from; it was a community of artists and musicians, the people I used to read about in magazines. Everyone appeared to be always smiling and happy, going to parties, wearing cool clothes, out with partners and getting drunk.

Everyone except me. Inside, I was still that too-thin, perm-haired, idiot teenager. An imposter. But I had to integrate. It just happened that this had to be with members of bands whose records I'd bought.

So, I reverted to my traditional coping mechanism: concentrate on something I know about and do it obsessively well. Something that gives me a reason to talk to other people, without them 'finding me out'. Then maybe the whole friendship process might just happen. Like magic.

So I became manager of the local musicians' Sunday football team.

It made sense to me. I watched more football than anyone I knew. I knew more than anyone I knew. And I used to think I could play it as well as anyone I knew but I hadn't totally appreciated, how tough it would be to do this well enough to impress people, who would then naturally become my friends. The singers, guitarists and drummers of London W11 didn't care as much as me that they needed to be on a football pitch, ideally in their kit, by 10.30 a.m. on a Sunday morning.

Particularly, if there was even a sniff that it might not be dry and sunny. At kick-off time there were hangovers, missing players, players still in their 'disco state', nine on the pitch, two on their way.

It did my head in! Managing a Sunday-morning football team was doing my head in!

But somehow it worked, but only because the opposition were often in exactly the same state as us.

The geeky kid who neatly tucked his jersey into his shorts when he practised alone in the park across from his house was now managing and playing with the likes of Damon Albarn (talks a good game), Hugh Grant (not a footballer), Phil Daniels (dynamic, midfield general), Jamie Theakston (our great goalkeeper), Gavin Rossdale (gave great lip and got into a punch-up with our own captain once because of it) and Billy Duffy of the Cult (legendary stories).

They might have been actors and musicians but I treated them as if they were professional footballers. I even went on a training course to obtain an FA coaching badge. I failed it.

That didn't stop me trying to coach this team of hungover band members, for whom this was meant to be a fun reason to get out of bed on a Sunday morning, and not more work.

The statistics at the end of the season were OK, though. We won some, drew some, lost some, but, most importantly for me, I had moved to a new area and hadn't totally embarrassed myself. I was on speaking terms with most people. They didn't think I was an idiot. They just thought I took things a little too seriously. That I could be a little intense perhaps.

Meanwhile, I had been devoting every other breath to managing Delphi to a publishing deal and Honeychild to a record deal to make an album. We talked to several producers and agreed on two Americans. And, best of all, because of the favourable currency exchange, we were going to record it in New York.

Wow!

The pursuit to prove everyone wrong continued.

Just after I'd got an application in for my first passport.

Sheldon Cooper is a fictional character, brilliantly played by Jim Parsons, in the TV series *The Big Bang Theory*. He is the archetypal nerd and perfectionist, but one with some insight into his 'condition'. Sheldon has a 'thing' about sitting in only one certain chair 'his seat', in the apartment he shares with his roommate, Leonard. In the pilot episode, Sheldon explains the rationale behind why that seat is his perfect seat, the only one he can sit in and why no one else should sit in it.

In the winter that seat is close enough to the radiator to remain warm, and yet not so close as to cause perspiration.

In the summer, it's directly in the path of a cross-breeze created by opening windows there and there.

It faces the television at an angle that is neither direct, thus discouraging conversation, nor so far wide as to create a parallax distortion.

I could go on, but I think I've made my point.

Advice to anyone thinking of befriending a perfectionist

All you've got to be aware of is, I probably take too many things a little too seriously. Other than that, I hope you'll find I'm not too different from your other friends.

I'm not the most forthcoming person in the room, but when we do actually get to talk I will be very interested in who you are and what really makes you tick. Probably, the most interested in the room actually.

I don't do small talk, I'm afraid. Likewise, I won't enjoy it if we happen to just bump into each other in the street; I might even cross the road to try to avoid you. It's because I only want you to see my best side, but I can't prepare perfectly for anything spontaneous. I don't want to disappoint you. Or anybody in fact.

If I do happen to say anything I don't think completely accurately reflects what I meant, I can worry about it for days. I'll probably try and bring it up in conversation again, so I can correct the misunderstanding that I think I could have caused. So, don't think me odd if I revisit a conversation you thought was finished.

Not surprisingly, I often feel misunderstood. Not many people know the real me.

As with many things in my life, I need to be in control, to make sure everything is just right. So, please excuse my rudeness if I keep my options open or suggest a different idea at the last minute. Please don't take it personally. It's not you; it's me.

I prefer it if I can be the one that suggests where we meet and what we do, but only because I would have thought about it longer than you and will only suggest somewhere if I think it will be perfect. Once we're under way, you might hear me make the odd little comment to reiterate, as much to myself as to you, that this certainly was the right choice.

After all that, I still might worry that you don't agree. If I do, that could ruin it for me. If you don't think it's perfect, please keep it to yourself. We'll happily remain friends, then. If you do have to say something, please excuse my occasional overreaction. It's nothing personal. I probably agree with you; it's just I'm frustrated with myself for not getting it right.

If we get through that, unfortunately I could still go off you – if you don't live up to my expectations, do something I think reflects badly on me, or aren't completely honest with me, I struggle to have any dishonesty in my friendships.

I never said it was easy being friends with a perfectionist. I've got standards to uphold. The standards of the entire bloody world unfortunately.

I like successful people. I'm interested to work out how you achieved it. Unless of course I don't think you deserve it. I won't say anything, but your success will just be proof anyone can do it, including me.

I do like it when people ask about me. Even if you don't ask, you'll probably hear all about me anyway because I can't stop myself trying to impress you. I hope you admire my achievements because I actually crave that. I'm aware I can come across as a show-off and some people might think I am a bit of a narcissist. I'm aware of it but if something that might impress you is on my mind I literally cannot stop myself saying it. Literally. Sorry.

The upside is you'll never have to listen to any bad stories about me. Unless, of course I've overcome something and moved on. Then, hopefully, you'll be really impressed by how I achieved that. (This book might just be a small example of this.)

Oh, one last little thing, please don't joke at my expense. I struggle to laugh at myself. As they say, many a true word is spoken in jest. I take everything you say literally, I'm afraid. I find a little too much room for misunderstandings in sarcasm and irony.

I know you'll think this surprising but I don't let many people into my life – not that I'm turning a queue of people away.

But now we've got to know each other, please stay. I will be your best friend; I won't gossip or lie to you. I will be your most loyal and trusted companion. I need good and honest people in my life.

I need friends.

AGE 28
Perfectionist Lover

In New York, the recording of the Honeychild album was going well. The band was in the studio with the producers. I was in a bar with my new passport and a girl.

Since I had what I considered to be the realistic pursuit of pop superstardom at the forefront of my life, relationships had always come a distant second. But for the last two years, I had been going out with a girl I had met at a gig. She had lived near my parents but became a nurse in London and we moved in together. We liked the same music and we spent a lot of our time seeing bands together.

Prior to that, I'd had a number of very short flings but felt we hadn't had enough in common to actually go out. The girls I met acted as though they wanted to progress things quickly, see me every night, stay over and then move in. I certainly wasn't up for that. 'I need my own space and time, sorry.'

I'd stupidly had an affair while I was on tour with the band in Germany, though. It was initially exciting. It was with someone who was cool, who seemed to like me. But I wasn't proud of myself. In fact, I hated myself. I hated living a lie, even though I was still 700 miles away from my girlfriend and hadn't yet had the chance to actually confess to the lie.

When I did return home, I was so nervous. I didn't think I could live one second without telling her the truth. Telling her exactly what I had done.

So, I told her on the doorstep as she opened the door to welcome me home.

Understandably, she was more than angry and upset. I'd let her down. I'd let myself down.

I was never going to be good enough at being a boyfriend.

I haven't had an affair since. I literally can't. Not that I have had much opportunity. I'd still never asked a girl out, never even asked one to dance, since that fateful night in a suburban club ten years earlier. Too embarrassing.

So, I certainly didn't exchange many words with my teenage pin-up, Debbie Harry, a few months later either, other than about her strong views on meat-eaters.

The Honeychild album turned out OK, and to promote it the record company paid for the band to go on tour supporting Debbie, the lead singer of Blondie, on a solo tour around Britain. It was sold out and set the band up for the release of their album.

Three weeks after, though, I bumped into the band in a pub, having a 'band meeting' without me. That wasn't a good sign.

Thirty minutes later they were in my flat, sacking me.

They didn't like that I'd agreed with our record label that the production on the album wasn't good enough. I was only telling the truth; it's the only way I could be. I just genuinely thought it needed to be better if we wanted to have a hit single. Like, my now former, girlfriend, they didn't appreciate the unfiltered honesty.

I hadn't managed to get Delphi a record deal, so I was now approaching the end of my twenties with no band to manage, no money, no girlfriend, and thanks to Ms Harry, a new commitment to myself – I'd become a vegetarian.

Advice to anyone thinking of dating a perfectionist

I do love going out of an evening. It gives me a deadline to get my work done by. If I don't have a deadline, there'd be a danger I could let my tasks run late into the night or, worse, not finish at all, leaving me to spend the night distracted and grouchy.

Before I can go out I need my head to be clear, so I can actually spend a few hours relaxing, away from the demands it's normally full of. I need all my tasks to be up to the stage where I think they should be, so I'm happy to let them leave my mind for a few hours. I've earned some time off.

Unfortunately, that also means I might 'occasionally' be late. I can't leave work until I've achieved what I'd committed myself to achieving earlier in the day, however much extra work might have come my way in the intervening hours.

So here we are finally standing outside the front door, coming to an agreement on where to go ... I'll just pop back inside, as I might have left the bathroom light on and I'll just grab a notepad, just in case I have five minutes to myself at some point.

We get to the pub. I realize this is slightly odd, but I like to sit next to my date. I'm more relaxed when I'm chatting side by side and don't have to look straight into the eyes of the person I'm with. Anyway, it also means we can both enjoy the best view, the one that creates the most conversation, people-watching the rest of the room.

When I know you won't notice, I'll drag one end of the table, just very slightly towards me, maybe one or two centimetres, so that it is parallel to my chair, which is slightly lower than I'd wish, so it's playing on my mind. I need to keep my back straight to be at the level I want to be over my food. I'm not totally relaxed yet, but I'm getting there.

While you're looking at the menu I'll just nip to the loo. I like to make sure I go before I eat. In fact, I don't just like to go – what am I talking about? I have to go. I don't ever sit down for a meal until I have done so.

I need to take all the time I have before someone comes over to take our order, to make sure I am going to order the right thing. Almost literally weighing up the ingredients of each dish in my mind, adding them to the mood I'm in, who I'm with and what I've got to do in the morning. Then working out which dish provides the perfect answer to that equation.

Now, everything is just right. I'm ready to enjoy this.

Oh, unless of course, the place is so quiet I can hear you crunching the food in your mouth, someone else scraping the cutlery on their plate or people either speaking loudly to their friend or their baby, as if their friend doesn't understand the same language or their baby was born deaf.

If none of that is happening, I'm good to go.

I just want everything to be just right.

You won't know I'm thinking most of that by the way, or at least I hope you won't. To you, I probably seem just slightly distracted. Please don't think it's because I'm annoyed with you for any reason. That will just frustrate me if you think that.

It's not you; this is just me. This is just the way I am.

Let's eat ... I'm looking forward to a relaxing night out.

What!? You want to go home with me now?

Before you commit to that, imagine all of the above going through my head while at the same time I'm completely naked.

Symptom: unfiltered honesty

Many perfectionists struggle to join in with gossip and bad-mouthing people behind their back while continuing to be friends with the subject of the gossip. It is living a lie. Perfectionists struggle to live any lie, unless they can completely convince themselves it is actually not a lie but the truth. This means they can also be too brutally honest for their own good and the good of their relationships.

While a perfectionist comes to terms with moderating their behaviour, accept they are just being honest and that this has nothing to do with their actual feelings.

Perfectionists see honesty as a good trait and simply as communication of a fact. They don't see honesty as having anything to do with expressing emotions.

Symptom: loneliness

A perfectionist shows more devotion to achieving perfection than to any person. They will often spend longer at work, where they can feel engrossed in the flow of work, than at home, or in environments they can't control. While they are in the middle of a task, it is often better to let them complete it without trying to attract their attention. Interruption will be unwelcome, often just leading to arguments.

A perfectionist's initial indifferent response to a distraction is often perceived as annoyance – with you. That leads to the standard question 'What's wrong?' and a real argument ensues. About what? Anything! But it's destructive, especially when the same thing happens year after year after year.

Many perfectionists struggle to share a genuine, loving relationship. They are too busy, too engaged, trying to achieve the perfection that they hope will result in you wanting a genuine, loving relationship with them.

It's a spiral that tragically leads to many relationship breakdowns and divorces. All due to the misunderstanding of what perfectionism really is.

AGE 29

All about the timing

Achieving success without perfection (2)

Marketing: companies are recognising that student consumers may stay brand-loyal in later life

Chasing future big spenders

By Helen Jones

THERE are a million students in the UK, but as a consumer group they are notoriously difficult to target.

The main problems are that students are fickle, influenced by rapidly changing fashions, and lead a relatively insular life, which revolves around work, dating and drink – although not necessarily in that order.

However, as students have an estimated spending power of £4bn a year, a growing number of companies are attempting to target effectively these consumers of tomorrow while they are in higher education.

One such company is Beatwax. It was set up by Chris Ward, who used to manage bands and organise tours to universities and colleges.

Beatwax began by organising university promotions for record companies, and this quickly expanded into video and film promotion. In the past two years, as companies have become aware of the value of the student market, the client range has broadened to include Bass, Cadbury and Virgin.

Mr Ward says that students are an ever-growing market. Universities and colleges of higher education are better attended than at any time in their history.

There has been a 20 per cent rise in enrolment in the past three years due to demographic changes and the trend for young people to opt for further study if they cannot find employment.

He is also keen to dispel the perception that students do not have any money. "With student loans, they have as much money to spend as they ever did. They are just further in debt when they leave higher education. But it doesn't stop them spending money on the clichéd things that students have always spent money on – drink, music, cigarettes and convenience foods."

Despite students' spending power, Mr Ward concedes that perhaps the easiest way to attract them is through free products or discounts. One of Beatwax's most recent campaigns has been for tea producer, Twinings. It has distributed 20,000 herbal tea sachets around universities and colleges in the expectation that if students try the product and like it, they will buy it on a regular basis and continue to do so after graduation.

Golden Wonder has also run a promotional campaign for its "Pots of the World" brand [illegible] is a more exotic version of that staple student fare, "Pot Noodles".

Beatwax targets advertising and promotions at students on their home territory. Mr Ward says: "They don't all watch the same television programmes or read the same newspaper – many of them don't read newspapers at all."

However, 86 per cent of all students read their university or college publications. Beatwax runs ad campaigns in these and has access to other on-site media such as campus radio stations and poster sites.

There are also growing opportunities to use video. As many as 85 colleges have mass-access video facilities – large multi-screen arrangements in bars, unions, refectories and discos.

Nearly all colleges also have their own on-site shop, which is often the only retail outlet nearby – particularly on campus sites. Beatwax organises in-store promotions, point-of-sale material and marketing campaigns for clients to increase sales of its stocked products.

Much of the marketing activity that Beatwax produces is particular to the student body and other consumers never see it. Mr Ward points out: "Companies can be more daring in the campaigns that they direct at students and often use more outrageous humour."

The company has organised a cross-promotion for the latest Hollywood blockbuster, *Naked Gun 33⅓ – The Final Insult*, and a number of sperm banks. Sperm banks are a traditional source of revenue for impoverished male students, and the film contains a scene set in such an institution. Beatwax is using this to advertise the film and to target potential donors.

"It is not something you could do generally, but you can be more controversial when marketing to students," Mr Ward says.

While sperm banks do not expect to attract students after graduation, Mr Ward says smart companies are realising the value "of getting them young" and retaining vital customer loyalty into salaried life.

Growing: universities and colleges are better attended than ever — Photograph by ROBERT PERRY

A newspaper feature on my new business

Although I was happy being able to just about afford to pay my bills and get by, with the loss of the government enterprise money I received for managing bands, I now urgently needed to earn some, so I could continue to do just that. The pursuit of success would need to be paused for a short time.

I had moved out from the flat share with Peter; his through-the-night songwriting sessions had turned his bedroom into a nightclub. I was now living in a tiny rented bedsit around the corner.

I was desperate for money, simply for food and rent, so I got a job as a cycle courier. But standing around for hours, waiting for the agency to call with a new job, was a complete waste of my life. So, at the end of the second day, I unpicked the logo off the courier bag, wrapped it up and gave it to my dad as his birthday present. It was all I could afford.

My old flatmate Fiona was by now all over the newspapers as the host of Breakfast TV and on exactly the same day I gave my dad the courier bag for his birthday, I turned on the TV to see Peter, performing one of the songs he'd been writing all night at our flat, 'Things Can Only Get Better'.

They obviously had for him. I needed to make them do the same for me. If two of my old flatmates could become successful, so could I.

I met a friend who worked at a record label, he suggested an idea for a new business, to promote bands through university DJs and campus newspapers and radio stations, to reach Britain's student population. They were a small but very important audience for the music industry.

We knew there would be some demand for the service but weren't sure how much. I thought we should give it a go. I had lots of bills to pay. And literally nothing to lose.

Again, I set myself to working all hours from my studio flat, on minimal money, on my own. I had to wait for my unemployment benefit to be paid, so I could afford to send a small brochure to record companies and the first client CDs out to universities. I put as much love and care into it as I had into unsuccessfully managing bands for the previous five years.

But this time, the same record companies did return my calls, inviting me in for meetings and paying me. Newspapers even wrote about what I was doing. The difference wasn't commitment to work – that was the same as it always was, 100 per cent full-on. No, the difference was the timing.

As I launched, the government announced that they were going to fund a huge increase in the number of college leavers going to university. The number of students was going to rise by at least 50 per cent. And I was sitting there as the one person, in a rented tiny studio flat, with the knowledge of, and rapidly growing expertise in, how to reach them.

The business grew as rapidly as the student numbers. I couldn't cope with the number of boxes turning up in the flat, so I rented a studio and was even able to afford to pay the goalkeeper from the musicians' football team to come and help.

I still wanted to manage bands. I'd only hit pause on that. I hadn't rationalized any reason to press stop. I was only doing this to earn a bit of money to tide me over, until I had enough to press play again.

Solution: be conscious of timing

The timing of when you launch a business is critical to its success, whereas spending endless weeks trying to make it perfect can be harmful. Too many businesses fail because the owner spends so long trying to perfect an idea that they miss the opportunity entirely and can only watch as someone else, with a half-formed product, gets it out into the market, evolves it with customer feedback and rides a wave of success.

When I'm looking into launching new projects now, I spend longer making sure the timing is right for the idea than trying to perfect it. If your idea doesn't match with the current news agenda, the media won't cover it. Potential customers live increasingly busy lives, with a decreasing amount of free time and money. If they are to notice your idea at all, it has to fit into their everyday life, and make that life better, today.

:(Part Three :)

Success and family life

AGE 30
Going travelling
Escaping the demand for perfection (3)

I was finally there, standing on the Great Wall of China, alone but for a few other backpackers. I'd been putting it off for years, too scared to go travelling on my own. There were too many things I couldn't control, too many uncertainties, too many worries, too many things I wouldn't know, mainly languages. In short, too much stress. This could go very wrong.

But if I hadn't acted out of character and booked that three-month backpacking trip around South-East Asia earlier in the year, I wouldn't have made it there at all. Having no bands to manage, nothing moving forward, I resorted to my default, running away from everything. But what I hadn't planned for was that in the last twelve weeks my little start-up business would actually start to do well: there were more clients, more staff, more office space, more products to mail out. I should have been in the office really.

But I had spent all the proceeds from my first payment to take me 5,000 miles away. I thought it would feel like a million. I had flown to Moscow and then spent an amazing eight days on the Trans-Siberian Express to Beijing. A day-long cycle ride out of town and I was there, standing on the Great Wall of China!

It was just me and the smallest backpack. Less stuff equalled less to worry about and less to be distracted by. I could just enjoy what I was doing for once. I loved it.

Out in the big world, I was in control of my own little one. It wasn't a world that anyone else wanted any sort of say in anyway. So, I could do exactly what I wanted. Exactly how I liked it. The adventure was far easier than making the decision to actually do it had been.

I travelled slowly to new places, meeting new people, tasting new food, experiencing new cultures. I loved being away from the old commitments, distractions and pressures. I could actually relax.

But I was also a little excited. For when I eventually made it to the airport for the flight back west, it wasn't taking me back to the stresses of my new office life. Instead, it was taking me to Greece.

Just three weeks before I left, three months earlier, I had met a girl who liked music and football as much as I did. I certainly didn't believe that would ever happen.

Despite spending the next three months apart, she had agreed to meet me in an Athens hotel at the beginning of an island holiday together. That was mad. That might have been more out of character for me than for her, though. It was the first time that I'd ever had thoughts for a girl that were stronger than my thoughts for proving everyone wrong.

Escaping the demand for perfection (3)

Travel, like all 'escapes', provides a respite from the demands of work, but it won't necessarily also provide the much more needed respite from the demands of perfectionism. You can all too easily take them with you, unless you consciously leave the mental baggage that causes you anxiety at home.

In the office or home, you need what you do, to be perfect. While travelling, that demand doesn't just go away. It goes away with you.

So, if you take too many things, book too many activities, make too many commitments, then you are equally likely to be distracted and worried about how well everything is going to go. You can ruin your own break with your too high expectations.

Escapes work best for perfectionists when you take as little physical, mental and emotional baggage with you as possible.

And don't make the common mistaken generalization of believing your holiday was good because everyone is friendlier abroad. They are the same as at home. It is you that is friendlier, because you have unburdened yourself of the demands you make on yourself.

Minimalist travel is one way to escape the demands, but the off-switch on your mobile phone can have much the same desired effect. Minimize the causes of anxiety in your life.

How you feel on holiday is how you can feel at home, work, anywhere, for the rest of your life. Understanding the root of your perfectionism will mean that you can stop carrying mental baggage everywhere you go.

Travel provides an escape, not the answer. If a perfectionist can understand their true mindset, they will no longer need to escape.

AGE 31
Meeting the *right* person

There she was, in the Athens hotel foyer – Helen, the girl who liked football. And not just football; she liked all sports. For our second date, I had taken her to see a play about my boxing hero, Muhammad Ali. We both loved it.

That was back at home, three months ago. Now, we endured a very nervous first few hours in the Athens hotel. Were each of us as we remembered? Did we really have that much in common?

Really? Are you sure?

Yes.

We took a ferry to the nearest island and found a lovely small apartment overlooking an idyllic harbour. Heaven for most people, but not for us two.

By coincidence, while we were there, Britain's two best boxers, Frank Bruno and Lennox Lewis, were fighting each other for the World Heavyweight Championship. It was live on sports channels around the whole world, except, it seemed, on this small Greek island.

We both wanted to see it. We debated the pros and cons for days, whether to check out of our hotel, get a ferry and exchange this island paradise where we were starting to fall in love for a sports bar in downtown Athens.

Finally, and with much gut wrenching, we agreed to stay. I loved the fact we were both keen to debate it properly and consider all the pros and cons before agreeing the correct answer. I liked this girl.

I grew up a loner, thinking that I was a weird geek and that no girl would ever like me.

Luckily for me, Helen was a weird Greek who had a fascination with geeky, loner types.

I'd never had so much in common with someone before:

We had both always loved football

Helen's father used to sneak her into matches with him under the turnstiles, while I was taking my dad, who had no interest in football, so I could get a lift home. Unfortunately, it wasn't a completely perfect match: I was going to see West Ham, while Helen was going to see Arsenal.

We were impressed by each other's record collections

Helen could name every player in the England World Cup squad on my 7-inch picture disc record. I was impressed, almost enough to ask her to marry me on that score alone. Helen was impressed that I owned a Barbra Streisand album but, much to her regret, assumed it was because I was in touch with my feminine side, and not just because someone had given it to me.

We both worked in the music industry

Helen was personal assistant to the boss of Parlophone Records, where she ordered copious amounts of flowers and sorted out everyone's huge expense claims. My job was to try to get promotional work on bands – from the boss of Parlophone Records.

We were both obsessed about the same people

We both had a fascination with people who could create amazing pieces of art, writing, music or acting but seem to have to bear their soul and sacrifice everything in the process, never compromising or stopping until they have achieved exactly what they set out to do. What makes them do that? What goes on behind the scenes in their personal life? They appear driven, but are they happy? We both liked people like that. We both admired them. We were both fascinated by perfectionists – from a distance.

We both worried about the same things
A strange one, but we bonded over our anxieties. I had obviously worried all my adult life about trying to avoid something bad happening. Helen did likewise. We could both worry about literally any likely impossibility, to the extent that, if any of them actually ever happened, we would have found ourselves on the front pages of the newspapers every single day. The only difference being that Helen worried that something bad might happen to her, whereas I worried that I might make something bad happen to somebody else.

Our families
We both came from traditional families, where our dads worked hard and our mums put the food on the table.

The only, minor, difference being mine was made up of five Brits, where I was the eldest son with two younger sisters, raised on a stiff upper lip and my mum's wisdom and cooking.

Helen's was made up of fifty-five Greeks, where she was the youngest daughter with two elder brothers, fourteen uncles and aunts, twenty-six cousins and eighteen nieces and nephews, raised around a hotbed of emotions, fiery disagreements, big hugs, lots of kissing and enough food to feed everyone, twice ... at least.

We had so much in common ... I even asked her to dance! But only after she had said 'I do' in front of a priest first.

I agonized. What if we aren't perfect for each other? Then what? I wouldn't be able to cope with being trapped in a marriage with the wrong person. I had been taught that you stay together, despite any arguments and differences. My parents would think I had failed if this marriage didn't work.

It wasn't worth thinking about.

The girl who liked football, with her father

Helen did like geeky, loner types. She liked watching and reading anything about them; musicians, artists, actors ... But would she actually like to spend her entire life with one that certainly wasn't doing anything worth watching or reading about?

It did feel like we were a perfect match. It felt like we were meant to be. But maybe those were slightly unrealistic expectations to have on your wedding day.

Symptom: fear of commitment

Perfectionists fear committing to anything, as, once they do, they need it be perfect. They agonize over every detail, needing to believe it can be perfect before they commit.

So, 'till death us do part'? That's the biggest commitment they can ever make.

The moment that the idea of the perfect relationship gets damaged – an argument over something they know they can't ever compromise on, often being an early warning sign – that's the moment the problems begin, when perfection is no longer possible. They need to do literally everything to get it back on track or give up altogether.

Nothing helped me and Helen when that moment arrived in our marriage. Nobody ever mentioned perfectionism.

AGE 32
A good day at work

We were back from our honeymoon and back to work. The number of clients who wanted to use our services, seemed to be never-ending. And they weren't just record companies anymore, but businesses that sold anything students might be interested in buying – video games, crisps, beer, chocolate ... even condoms.

And I learned fast. Businesses that didn't sell music could afford to pay far more for marketing to students than those that did. I was generating a whole lot more income than this stopgap money-making idea had been created to do, which was to cover the cost of my food and rent.

Student numbers were growing, and so was the crest of the wave on which we were surfing. Any potential competition had been caught off guard. The timing had been right; we were the only business offering this service. All our clients were new to me, but there was no pressure on me to understand what they did; they were paying us to understand all about what students did.

People liked my ideas: the more creative they were, the better. It was an exciting and fun time. This was like inventing game ideas, but getting paid for it. Ha, I thought, that will show my old art college lecturers and those oh-so-arty students.

I had a good income for the first time in my life. Helen and I even started going to the occasional restaurant. Paying to eat out had never been on my agenda before. We eventually bought our first flat, a small two-bedroom basement in West London. It meant Helen leaving the immediate reach of her parents in East London. She struggled with that.

For the first time as an adult, though, I actually felt valued, so this was a small cloud in a very sunny year.

Symptom: trapped by the trappings of success

It took me too many years – putting off friendships and relationships, so I could build my businesses bigger and bigger – to realize that this had been the best time I could ever have in an office – when it was just about a good idea, at the right time, and with just a small team. You feel valued, are enthusiastic, and can enjoy the novelty of everything as well as the income; you are free to work from anywhere, be in control of your own time, and can make quick decisions and action them quickly.

Work never gets more enjoyable than that for perfectionists.

But perfectionists don't start businesses for them to be enjoyable; they start them to grow them. The more successful they become, the more they will gain admiration and the happier they believe they will be. Perfectionists are trapped by the idea that the trappings of success will finally set them free.

But when a start-up idea turns into a business, it results in them having to change their role: from the enjoyable entrepreneurial one they started out with, to becoming the 'boss' – a manager of other people, of timekeeping, of income and expenditure, of red tape …

Many generally work to grow their business in order to sell it, so they get a big payday, with the proviso that they contractually need to stay on a few more years, often in a less happy environment, due to their now lacking control. But they go through it because they believe that at some point in the future they will finally be happy and able to enjoy life.

I was happy and enjoying life now. Unfortunately, I didn't realize that at the time.

Perfectionists are completely oblivious to the happiness possible in the everyday, while they pursue the end-goal they have fixed in their mind.

AGE 33
Perfectionist parent

There were five weeks to go. Five weeks to attend the important antenatal classes that would teach us 'how to parent'. How to take a new-born baby and make sure it could eat, sleep, feel our total love for it and grow up happy and contented every single day of its life. Only five weeks of Helen's pregnancy left – to go from knowing absolutely nothing to knowing absolutely everything about raising a happy child. One that would never forget it was born good enough.

That had been the discussion in the pub five hours earlier. As it turned out, to learn all of that, we actually only had five minutes.

It was 1 a.m. We were in an operating theatre, fluorescent lights blazing, the radio blaring, and Helen was about to undergo an epidural, followed by gas and air, followed by an emergency caesarean operation. Five hours earlier, her waters had broken and, after some rushed packing and an urgent drive to hospital, the nurse confirmed that the baby's head was indeed engaged and Helen was already well dilated.

Five minutes earlier, the doctor confirmed that it wasn't actually the head that was engaged, but the bottom. The baby was breech. Thus, we had the bright lights and a very dodgy Simply Red song on the radio and not the beautiful birthing moment we had been hoping to share together in five weeks' time.

We were both out of our depth and petrified. Helen was flat out on the operating table, I was crouched beside her. Our noses were touching, as we clung to each other, one side of a green screen that had been erected halfway down her body.

A few minutes longer of frantic, urgent action than we would have liked and we heard a cry, then another, then a full burst of screaming. Molly was here. Five weeks early and incredibly tiny but with lungs made of iron.

While they were both wheeled away, Helen to rest and Molly to bathe under a special anti-jaundice light, I went to the bathroom, closed a cubicle door, sat on the seat and just sobbed.

My chest was heaving with years of withheld emotions. The real, imperfect me, fighting its way out from under the perfect front I tried to present to everyone.

I had never dreamed such a moment could ever happen. I never believed that someone would love me, enough to want children with me, that I would be man enough to provide them, that I would ever feel so much outpouring of love.

This wasn't falling in love because we had things in common.

This was falling in love because I was in love.

For the first time in my adult life, I felt unconditionally right. I felt genuine love for Helen and Molly. I understood what people meant when they say 'I love you'. I had a glimpse of what life was meant to be about.

It was unconditional love.

It was overwhelming.

Solution: increased support for expecting parents

The British NHS offers sixteen hours of classes in which to teach expectant parents about the physical and mental wellbeing of the mother-to-be and the baby – that's if, as they warn, they are not 'sold out'. This is nowhere near long enough to impart all the relevant knowledge that can best help new parents raise happy, well-rounded children who will be able to cope with the constant demands they will face to be perfect. That goes for the parents, too. A whole industry has grown up to fill that gap and capitalize on parents' doubts as to whether they will be good enough mothers and fathers by promising them that they can be by buying this book, that product or some other piece of rubbish.

The English writer and theologian **G. K. Chesterton** defended the amateur against the professional, especially when it came to 'the things worth doing', in his 1910 book *What's Wrong with the World.*

Chesterton foresaw the dilemma of day care and the working mother, that children would end up being raised by 'professionals' rather than by 'amateurs'. And here we must understand 'amateur' in its truest and most literal meaning. An amateur is someone who does something out of love, not for money. She does what she does, not because she is going to be paid for her services and not because she is the most highly skilled, but because she wants to do it. And she does 'the things worth doing' that are the things closest and most sacred to all humanity – nurturing a baby, teaching a child the first things, and, in fact, all things.

AGE 34
Maintaining a stiff upper lip

We were at Bournemouth Football Club stadium. It was Molly's first football match. She was only six months old, wrapped tight and warm by Helen, even though it was the height of summer, but it was obviously important she saw West Ham before she saw Arsenal! Even if it was just a meaningless friendly match. But hey, it was a sunny day at the seaside. Our baby was feeling sand and sea on her feet for the first time, as well as watching football. It was a big day in Molly's life.

Unfortunately, it was also a big day in Helen's life.

It was good to be out and about. It had been a stressful first six months of life, not that Molly knew that. She was fine. But the worry about ensuring that she was breathing, eating, sleeping and getting enough milk pushed Helen to the edge too often for her own good health. The baby being born five weeks early, jaundiced and underweight affected Helen's health more than it did Molly's. With her real struggle to breastfeed, her mental health appeared to be deteriorating faster than Molly's physical health was improving.

I didn't know what the answer was, though. I had no experience or knowledge of this. As Helen often accurately observed, 'You're no help.'

I just wanted everything to be all right.

Helen had been due back at work after three months' maternity leave. So, we had found a great nursery around the corner, and Helen dropped Molly there every morning. That lasted two months. Neither of us liked leaving Molly with strangers, not knowing what she was doing every minute, every second of her life. Not knowing how well she was integrating, eating, sleeping or even just breathing.

The business was doing well now. Well enough for us to test out if we could afford for Helen to look after Molly full-time. It seemed to help, and it was only then, when she was six months old, that Helen admitted to me, to herself even, that she had struggled to bond with our first child. That maybe she had been struggling with post-natal depression.

I was only a bloke. I knew nothing.

Helen totally agreed.

So, instead of working through it with me, Helen turned to her mother and father for the love and support I was meant to be providing. I made myself useful in the only way I knew how to, I stayed at work longer.

So, that weekend, it was good to be out and about at the seaside on a sunny day. Things were starting to look up. West Ham were winning.

While we queued for a half-time cup of tea, the tannoy announced 'a phone call for Helen Ward'. We found a helpful steward, and Helen took the call in the tea shack.

The first I had any idea of what it was about was when Helen dropped the phone and then fell to the floor, struggling to breathe.

It was her brother. Her parents had just returned early from their annual summer trip with relatives in Cyprus because a doctor had suggested that might be advisable for Bob, Helen's father. He'd just been for a hospital appointment and had ended up being admitted and then diagnosed with late-stage lung cancer. He had then had a heart attack, to compound everything.

Helen's dad was dying. And she'd just been told that, in the tearoom at a football ground, halfway through a meaningless match, a hundred miles from home, with baby Molly on her lap.

We were in the car in minutes, back in London in hours and waiting by the phone for the next month. Until Helen's dad, my father-in-law, Molly's grandfather, the beloved head of a very large Greek family, died.

The next months, the rest of the year, was a nightmare. Helen, having lost her father and struggling with post-natal depression. Me, just saying and doing the wrong things. All the time.

I wanted to help but I didn't know what to do. I didn't have any answers but I couldn't admit that. I couldn't ask anyone for help with directions, so I was unlikely to be able to ask anyone how I could help my wife.

So, I just made a mess of it. I tried maintaining a stiff upper lip, suggesting everything will be all right, arranging days out to take her mind off of everything. I went through the whole range of inappropriate responses. Anything to avoid being open, honest and admitting I didn't know what to do and that I too was scared.

It just resulted in us arguing and Helen relying more on her mother and less on me. I was struggling because Helen was struggling. I needed her to be all right. I just couldn't do anything right. It was 'doing my head in'. I was rubbish at being a parent and partner.

A general election came along, and Tony Blair's New Labour landslide victory took place to the soundtrack of my old flatmate Pete's bloody song 'Things Can Only Get Better'. The whole of Britain was happily singing along while Helen and I could only hope that things would.

Unfortunately, it was also a very badly timed reminder that I was closer to the genuine success I needed through work than I was to making a success of fatherhood. So, I did what I thought was best for Helen, Molly and me: I went back to putting all my energies into building the business.

I needed to escape my own home, be somewhere else, where my emotions played no role, somewhere I knew what to do, where I could make things right.

Symptom: stifled emotions

Withholding emotions and maintaining a stiff upper lip in difficult times has traditionally been seen as a trait of men. It is not exclusively a male trait, but many boys who develop perfectionism into adulthood are taught that displaying emotion and vulnerability can be seen as a sign of failure. That, in the eyes of their father, it's the failure to have grown into a 'real' man.

So, perfectionists avoid displaying any outward signs of weakness and can hide almost any emotion, apart from frustration and anger. This obviously makes perfectionists appear uncaring, aloof, arrogant, stuck up, robotic and unemotional – all the nice things I was accused of being by Helen. Inside, though, they are often in complete emotional turmoil, stressing that they can't help and don't know the answers, while not being able to admit it.

They feel as vulnerable as the person they are trying to help, while at the same time trying to maintain control of everything around them. Which is why, when someone looks to a perfectionist for emotional support, they are more likely to receive 'technical', matter-of-fact advice. It's their safe default – and it's more for their own wellbeing than that of the person they're supposed to be supporting.

AGE 35
Perfectionist boss

Sticking to the one thing I was good at – work – meant the business did continue to grow. We moved to an office block that had a lift, receptionist and cleaners – three things I never thought would ever be part of my life. We were growing into a proper, successful marketing agency. I still hadn't rationalized to myself that I shouldn't be managing bands. It was still in my head, at the top of my to-do list, to become a proper, hopefully successful, band manager.

My job wasn't to generate new ideas anymore, though. Now it was to generate enough money to pay for everyone else to generate ideas. As the business grew, my enjoyment of it declined.

By then there were twenty of us and expectations had risen, not from staff or clients but inside my own head.

With managing bands on hold and fatherhood going badly, the business had become the route through which I could prove I was good enough. It was no longer about doing it just to pay the bills; I now needed it to pay for an increasingly bigger home and better food on both the kitchen and restaurant tables. So Mum and Dad would be proud of what I was achieving and Helen's Mum would be proud of the life her daughter was making with me.

I was managing people to do the job I had loved, and to do my job less well than me because none of them were as obsessed about getting it as right as me. My job was now to make sure there was enough new work for them to do, that they turned up on time and spent all day doing it, before they went back home again. But not before time.

I hated the person I'd become – the one who had all the controlling traits of a horrible boss:

1. I couldn't delegate.
2. I micro-managed.
3. I set impossible deadlines.
4. I didn't forget a thing.
5. I obsessed about details and lost sight of the bigger picture.
6. I never said 'no' to any clients, in case they never returned.
7. I rarely complimented anyone, unless they exceeded my impossibly high standards.
8. I made detailed lists of literally everything.

I was aware that not all this was good, but I couldn't stop myself. I didn't just need my work to be perfect, I needed everyone else's work to be perfect, too.

I succeeded, though only in making myself lonely. I pretended to be enthused whenever anyone knocked on my office door.

I didn't know how honest any of my office relationships were. All the staff were nice to me, but surely that was just because I was responsible for deciding the size of their pay packets and promotion? I was nice to all our clients, but I believed they thought that was because they were responsible for awarding us paid projects.

I didn't even know how honest any of the work I was doing was.

We did some sampling promotions for Diamond White, a premium cider. The client told us, if we ran out, the easiest way to get more was to go and buy the much cheaper ASDA own-label, two-litre cider bottles. Inside the much cheaper bottle was the same cider.

We ran a poll to find out which political leader students preferred – old-fashioned Conservative leader William Haig or 'man of the moment', Prime Minister, New Labour's Tony Blair? Obviously, they said Tony Blair. I thought no newspapers would be interested in running that story. So, we reversed the results and informed the media. They printed pages of editorial about how Tony Blair was losing his appeal to students.

Don't believe everything you read … or drink.

I didn't like Mondays anymore – they meant I was about to start another week of not being myself.

I'd given up believing in anything I was doing. None of it felt honest.

But I could no longer separate who I really was from the job I was doing. The job defined who people thought I was. It wasn't the real me, but I was trapped. Without this job I would be a nobody. With this success I was someone. Someone else. Someone in a spiral of loneliness.

Where did I take all this stress and anxiety? How did I rid myself of it?

Obviously, I took it straight home, through the now slightly more expensive front door, to the slightly bigger kitchen and the slightly nicer table, to the larger toddler's bedroom and finally to our bedroom, complete with new en-suite bathroom.

There was no hiding place from my stress, for anybody I loved.

Being a perfectionist boss is a lonely life. Being a perfectionist boss who's not talking to his wife was an even lonelier life.

Deservedly, there was no escape for me neither. I couldn't sleep.

Cause: achievement culture

The success-at-all-odds culture we now have is due to the natural development of neoliberalism in the age of the internet. Anything is possible by anybody. Look! The success of about a dozen internet multi-billionaires proves it. If they can do it, so can anyone, so can you.

Making a good living is no longer enough. Unless you are first to launch, or the biggest to sell, any success is no longer deemed enough for entrepreneurs. They are pumped up with motivating messages that life is no longer about them personally, no longer about happiness; it's about what they achieve.

Steve Jobs, the founder of Apple, was a notorious perfectionist whose behaviour negatively impacted not only his colleagues and employees but his friends and family, too. The following is an extract from an article by Rebecca Greenfield in *The Atlantic.*

Steve Jobs, Apple's late, lamented leader, was an adamant perfectionist but he was also more than a little crazy. From visionary to 'evil genius,' Jobs was both of these things, but most of all he was a 'tweaker,' someone who made bad ideas better. His gift lay in taking what was in front of him, the tablet with stylus, and ruthlessly refining it. This ruthless refinement is what made Jobs a genius, always perfecting designs until they popped out as perfect little iProducts.

But it also made him a little crazy, not always for the better.

Perfectionism plagued Jobs. It pushed him to not only make the iDevices we cherish, but to make unreasonable decisions. His obsession with detail, meant that the company took more than three years to develop the original Macintosh.

At times this constant striving for perfection demonstrated an almost endearing Larry David-esque neuroticism. 'He sits in a restaurant and sends his food back three times. He arrives at his hotel suite in New York for press interviews and decides, at 10 P.M., that the piano needs to be repositioned,' writes Malcolm Gladwell.

But it didn't stop at these harmless incidents. It pushed him to both hurt himself and others. Others have pointed to Jobs' terse behaviour with his employees. Some recalled him as 'rude, dismissive, hostile, spiteful,' writes Gawker's Ryan Tate, who discusses the manipulation Jobs used to 'inspire' his workers.

continued ...

Yet, Jobs went beyond the pushy boss, who blows off the handle. 'He screams at subordinates,' writes Gladwell and once told his public-relations assistant that her suit was 'disgusting.' He couldn't handle anything less than perfection, and often took it out on others.

The mental capacities that led Jobs to perfect computers and phones didn't stop at his inventions, but seeped into all aspects of his life. Jobs approached even the most mundane tasks, like picking out a washing machine, with the same thoughts of perfection in the back of his mind.

'We spent some time in our family talking about what's the trade-off we want to make. We ended up talking a lot about design, but also about the values of our family. Did we care most about getting our wash done in an hour versus an hour and a half? Or did we care most about our clothes feeling really soft and lasting longer? Did we care about using a quarter of the water? We spent about two weeks talking about this every night at the dinner table. All for a washing-machine.'

AGE 36
Behind every successful perfectionist ...

It started, like many of my ideas at work, when I flicked through a magazine or website and come across something that captured my attention. This one happened to be in a small computer magazine and was about a new website that could potentially reunite old school classmates. I thought it was a great idea and I wanted us to do the public relations for it.

Luckily, the owners agreed to my idea to market 'Friends Reunited' as if it was purely a small homespun operation, run by a couple from their kitchen table, without an office or a suit in sight. I believed the public would trust Steve and Julie, half of the ownership team. It worked a storm. Twelve million people in the UK joined up, and the postman beat a daily path to the Pankhurst's front door with bags of membership fees. TV crews hung around the back door, wanting to interview Steve and Julie about the phenomenon they supposedly ran from their cosy kitchen.

Months of front pages and TV interviews followed. Friends Reunited was an enormous success, reuniting millions of old friends, creating new marriages, a lot of new babies and a business worth over a hundred million pounds. I spent all day and night on it, but not all in the office and not much of it from my own kitchen. There were new clients to meet, speeches, awards nights and parties to attend.

At last.

I needed to capitalize on this moment to achieve more, win bigger clients and get more media coverage. This could be the moment I've dedicated my life working towards. Proving to everyone I was actually good at things, that I was good.

Good enough to run a successful business, but not good enough to contribute to a happy home though.

By now our second child, Bob, had been born. Again, it was a real bolt to my very core. A girl and a boy. A boy! Me, a father to my own son!

'I am your father, Bob.'

But the same problems that had occurred during Molly's first year reappeared, with Helen feeling more than stressed by the baby and less than supported by me.

At work, things were going well, but at home the complete opposite was happening again. So, once again, I was spending more time in the office, where people were impressed with what I was doing, rather than who I was and it was, as ever, an escape from the real me, the vulnerable new parent.

I wasn't 'me', but I could make everything right. I needed that more.

At home, I was struggling with something that had drawn me towards Helen only five years earlier, her close-knit family: my traditional English arm's-length, non-tactile childhood, versus Helen's huge Mediterranean family of warm, welcoming Greek Cypriots.

I had been taught that happiness came from building a home for one's immediate family, working hard when I was not there to provide, and working hard when I was at home to help. We don't need anyone else, thank you!

That's not how my Greek in-laws were raised, however. Meals are spent together with whichever friends, family members and neighbours happen to be in your kitchen at the time, and babies are raised by whichever female family member happens to be in the home. The father's sole contribution is to provide for the family, like all good Greek fathers do.

I struggled to cope with only playing this small role in my own home; it went against everything I believed was the right way a home should operate. That helped me justify to myself that my best role was working all hours, even when I didn't need to. And to enjoy the success, after hours. It was the perfect distraction from my imperfect home life.

In my house I was playing a bit-part in my own life. I had no control over doing anything the way I needed to, exactly how my father would want me to do it. I couldn't see that I was being in anyway unreasonable by not compromising on my belief that I should have some say, some control.

So, that's how it started – or ended. I was working long hours and didn't want to disturb Helen or the babies, or Helen's mum, and so I began sleeping in the spare room. It was a slippery slope and in the end I moved out of my home – the one I had worked all my life towards building.

I was leaving the one thing that was destroying both of us, our relationship, but at the same time leaving the two things that were my whole foundation, our children.

I rented a two-bedroom flat around the corner. Helen was good in agreeing to share the care of the children with me. They could stay at the house and the flat equally. That helped me enormously, as I could now compartmentalize my life. Half the time I was in control of work; the other half I was in control of my home and the children. I saw positives in that situation.

I wanted the flat to be as homely as possible, so I bought a big new TV. That's the quick win in this situation, isn't it? I dropped it in the middle of the road while I was struggling to unload it from the car. It smashed to pieces.

What was far worse, though, was receiving lawyer's emails, while I was sitting at my desk at work, entitled 'Access to Molly & Bob'. This felt like the worst injustice I had suffered in my life and I couldn't do one single thing about it. Every time I got an email, my heart, my whole body, dropped to the floor. In my goldfish-bowl office I was drowning.

I had rationalized to myself that this new set-up could work, but my heart, the real me, couldn't be kept quiet. It was still in there.

And it was depressed. I was depressed.

What's the point?

What's the fucking point?

Consequences: mental health issues

Just as we have social media stars selling perfect lives to teenagers, we now have the same with business founders. Tech 'gurus', with their hustle or 'struggle porn', are promoting the idea that the 'perfect life' – or their idea of such a life – is attainable by anyone, through endless, nonstop work.

I have yet to meet a founder who has a budget for self-care or who takes guilt-free vacations. In almost every other skilled industry there is recognition that people have a right to take care of themselves and that a little bit of self-care actually leads to a more productive workforce. Investors, founders and poorly trained middle managers all perpetuate a myth in the startup ecosystem that the only way to be successful is to grind yourself inexorably to the bone.

If everyone is willing to seek help and take care of themselves, it creates a company-wide habit that enables everyone to thrive. A healthy culture will pay for itself a thousand times over in recruitment, lower turnover and happier, more productive people.

The following is an extract from an article by **Jake Chapman** at techcrunch.com. It tells of the terrible price paid by entrepreneurs in terms of their mental health:

While national mental health statistics are troubling, they are downright terrifying for entrepreneurs. According to a study by Michael Freeman, entrepreneurs are fifty percent more likely to report having a mental health condition, with some specific conditions being incredibly prevalent amongst founders.

Business Founders are:

2X more likely to suffer from depression

6X more likely to suffer from ADHD

3X more likely to suffer from substance abuse

10X more likely to suffer from bi-polar disorder

2X more likely to have psychiatric hospitalization

2X more likely to have suicidal thoughts.

As Michael Freeman writes, mental health is as essential for knowledge work in the 21st century as physical health was for physical labor in the past. Creativity, ingenuity, insight, brilliance, planning, analysis, and other executive functions are often the cognitive cornerstones of the breakthrough value created by entrepreneurs.

Depression, anxiety and mood disorders all actively work to undermine founder performance. They often contribute to burnout, co-founder conflict, toxic company culture, increased employee turnover, an inability to hire top talent, an inability to 'show up' for important meetings and pitches and poor decision making in general. According to Noam Wasserman at HBS, 65 percent of failed start-ups fail for avoidable reasons like co-founder conflict. All of these experiences are exacerbated when founders are in a time of high mental and emotional strain.

AGE 37
Behind every rich perfectionist ...

Work harder. Work longer. That's the way to deal with depression. Don't actually confront it, or talk about it with anyone else.

The success of Friends Reunited resulted in more of everything – work, red tape, money, travel. More things that conveniently kept me from my family.

At work I was talking to the rich and successful.

At home I was talking to lawyers.

I couldn't carry on like this. I only wanted to show those people that wrote me off that I was good enough. I never wanted everything that went with that, the stress of living an entire life not true to who I really was.

I needed to stop it. I needed to run away from it all, as I always did. My solution: sell the business. That, I thought, was the only way to escape the nonstop demands that were slowly killing me.

So, I sent an email to some larger companies in the same sector saying my business was for sale. A few got back to me, and following a year of long meetings, thorough investigation of our accounts (not fun), a lot of lows and near misses, I eventually sold the business, with the proviso I continued to work there for a further three years to hand it over.

I became what I certainly considered rich. Certainly beyond the wildest dreams of a geek with no qualifications and permed hair. Mum and Dad sent me a 'congratulations' card. I think they were impressed. Not as much as I thought they might be, though, or as I hoped.

Helen's lawyer sent me another letter.

My complete and utter overriding feeling, though, was of complete relief. It was over; I will be able to stop pretending. I could handle three more years. It would be different from what I had done before, but at least I could now see a bright light at the end of the darkness. The bright light coming from the sheet of clean white paper, the new page, on which I could create a new idea and business plan on – my next project. One that I wouldn't allow to create the same stresses …

We became part of a larger group, with offices in Los Angeles and global film industry clients. This wasn't just different; it was a different planet. For the first few months I was just an observer, and because I didn't need to pretend I was someone I wasn't, my stresses lifted. I was a fly-on-the-wall of a planet full of very rich, very successful and even very famous people.

I wanted to share all this with someone. Someone who would appreciate the same geeky observations of the rich and famous as me, someone who I had a lot in common with.

Helen and I started sharing texts again. Nice texts, funny texts.

I started to have meetings in LA and manage movie parties in Cannes. That made Helen laugh – a geeky loner trying to organise cool parties!

Back on Planet Earth, we were getting on. I don't think either of us thought that me moving out was going to be the real end of our family. We always had too much in common, and we had only added to that with our two children.

I moved back home.

As I could now see a permanent route out of the office, I could put my energies into being the perfect husband instead. All we needed was the perfect home, a place into which I could put the money I had made from the sale.

We found it.

The house had recently been owned by a well-known designer and was 'quite nice' (me) 'perfect' (Helen). It backed onto a nice park, and the master bedroom had an en-suite bathroom that was bigger than our existing bedroom.

But, as the estate agent informed us – though only after we'd spent an hour looking around Helen's perfect home – there had already been an offer and it had been accepted. A dispiriting evening and a sleepless night followed, I knew how much Helen would have loved it.

But once I set my mind on something … At 9 a.m. sharp I rang the estate agent and asked what would happen if we matched the offer. Five minutes later he called back. The owners were keen to sell quickly, so would sell to the first people who could complete the purchase. We were in with a chance.

I rang a surveyor and solicitor whose opinions I trusted. Both went to work for a few hours before I got calls to say that, essentially, everything was good – the house was in good condition; it needed a little work but that wouldn't cost too much. The paperwork was all fine.

At 5 p.m. I left my office, cycled over to the solicitor's and signed contracts, with agreement to move in one month later. I cycled home.

'I've bought that house.'

'Which house?'

'The house. The one we saw yesterday'.

Helen didn't believe me. So I made a call and we walked round to see what was going to become our perfect home.

Within six months I was back sleeping in the spare room. A slightly bigger, ideal home-type spare room, but still a spare room. However much we enlarged the house, however much we improved the fixtures and fittings, however much money we had in the bank, none of it changed our relationship for the better.

Living in different houses, ones we had full control over, we could both be funny and flirty but living in the same house, where we were fighting over control of everything, these were the last two things we were able to be.

We just argued about the same things, time and time again, year after year, house after house. What kept us apart were the exact same, pathetically small differences that we couldn't see each other's view on, couldn't compromise over, or just consider, even for one moment, that we might not be right about.

I obviously concluded that, as we now had everything we could ever want, that it must be because I did a stressful job and Helen was stressed with the kids.

It was just normal. Just normal to have everything you've ever dreamed of, except simple joy, happiness and contentment.

Understanding: success and money don't bring happiness

Why doesn't success make perfectionists feel ultimately 'right'? Feel that people are proud of them? Make them contented and happy? This was what they put off enjoyment and friendships for, to reach this moment, when they will be finally sure that everyone is impressed with the person they've become, with what they've achieved.

Have they wasted their time? Have they wasted their life?

Yes.

Perfectionists often become unhappier as they become more successful. More success simply results in them being able to see even bigger things that they might be able to achieve. The child who only wants to be loved is lost in the pursuit of something bigger and better.

Success brings admiration, but only love can bring happiness.

Jim Carrey, actor, comedian, screenwriter, musician and painter, learned the lesson outlined in this chapter the long way:

Getting to the place where you have everything everybody has ever desired and realizing you are still unhappy is a shock when you have accomplished everything you ever dreamed of, and more, and then you realize, 'My gosh, it's not about this.'

I wish for everyone to be able to accomplish those things so they can see that.

AGE 38
Counselling

So, here we were, back at the start of this story, with a marriage counsellor.

Magazines were writing about my successes. Helen was talking about my failures. And while she was at it, also about my lack of most emotions – especially empathy.

Helen had said it all before. But now we were boring someone else, a counsellor we thought might be able to help us understand each other. Someone who could help us stop arguing with each other. Someone who could just help us be happy and relaxed together.

I was spending all day, every day, talking to new clients and new staff. I spent all evening, every evening, in silence, unable to say a word to Helen, in case it opened up an old argument.

I couldn't give up on us, though. Nor could Helen. We literally couldn't. We had both been raised with the lesson that you stayed together, even if you had fundamental differences. Or, in our case, even really minor ones.

And I hadn't just seen the facts, I'd torn them out of magazines: 'Married people are happier people', 'Married people live longer', 'Second marriages are not as happy as first ones', 'Kids raised in broken homes are more likely to suffer mental health issues.' This was proof enough for me. We had to try everything to make this work.

So, we went on a mission, to find that 'someone'. Someone we could both speak to, who could save us, from ourselves and from each other.

Not much to ask, surely?

Relate marriage guidance

We'd never done anything like this before – we were sitting in a tiny, soulless office with a woman facing us who, it seemed to me, could only say one line: 'What would you like to talk about today?'

'We'd like some help, please. We'd like you to guide us through our issues, so that we can understand ourselves and each other better, or even just enough, so that we can live together happily and, most importantly, raise our kids in a loving, supportive and non-argumentative environment. Please?'

'Yes. But what would you like to talk about today?'

It didn't feel like we really reached anything below the surface. We didn't have any problems with surface issues. Superficially, we had everything in common; it was the stuff that you couldn't see that was the issue.

So, after each nice session of agreeing about surface issues together, we'd make love.

Our relationship didn't get much better ... but Helen got a lot bigger. She became pregnant again. I wrote to Relate to inform them and thank them for their services.

No one, at any meeting we ever had, ever mentioned perfectionism or OCPD.

Going to church

We started going to the local church, simply because it was something we could agree to do together for the sake of the kids. After a few weeks, a friend told me about an amazing vicar who was going to launch a new, more contemporary church nearby.

I went alone and agreed: he was great, speaking common sense about contemporary issues. The following week Helen came too, though against her wishes, but within ten minutes she was in tears, as she realized that this felt more like a warm and welcoming home than our own did.

It was a real help, a community of genuinely good people, amidst the competitive, consumerist city we lived in. We were both unsure that religion was for us, but the community certainly were. It didn't solve our issues but it gave us one more thing we had in common and could do together.

A love languages course

We did a course about 'love languages', the principle being that there are five ways in which people show their love for one another: words of affirmation, acts of service, giving gifts, physical touch and committing quality time.

You need to show your partner you love them through the 'love language' they want (need, even), the way your partner most understands you are doing something loving for them and not the way you need to feel loved. Unless you both feel loved in the same way, if you show it the way you like to receive it, your partner will most likely not appreciate what you do as a sign of your love.

For example, I bought Helen bars of chocolate and booked nice places to go out, but she simply saw that as normal marriage stuff, not that I was trying to do something loving for her. This is also why, when she bought me some chocolate but then ate it herself, I stupidly felt unloved.

Something so pathetically small can have such a big impact.

We both agreed with the idea but neither of us were good at making the effort required. It would need us to break lifelong habits, and it seemed almost as though we didn't love each other enough to make the effort that would require.

The Hoffman Process

Helen thought, or, far more likely, I informed her, that her relationship with her mother was closer than ours was, and that she needed to understand why that was.

The Hoffman Process was a week when Helen was meant to go away, leave every piece of technology and access to the outside world behind, and make a vow to herself as to how she was going to move forward with her most important relationships.

I could tell Helen wasn't as immersed in it as the organizers would have liked, though, but that was actually a good thing for us. She rang me halfway through the week to discuss a football final, which she had managed to sneak out and listen to on the car radio.

Helen thought the course did help her recognize some co-dependency traits she had with her mother. But that certainly didn't mean she now wanted to be closer to her unemotional husband than to her loving mother.

Our children

There were certainly times when we stayed together because of our now three children, beautiful Rose having joined Molly and Bob in the bad-marriage firing line.

Neither of us could handle not living 24/7 with the most important people in our lives but it meant we had to always walk a tightrope – between minimizing the damage we would cause them by separating, or the damage we were causing by staying together.

Most of our endless, repetitive arguing seemed to boil down to being about how each of us were raised and what we believed to be the correct way to raise our children.

We were judging each other's parenting decisions in the same way our parents had judged us, which wasn't helpful. We were both taught there was only one correct way of doing things, so it was impossible we could both be right. One of us had to be wrong, and, for the benefit of our children, I felt it was important that we identified which one of us that was exactly.

Compromise

We both liked to control family life, which not surprisingly led to more tension than laughter. So, we agreed to just take control of different things: Helen, of the things we *used* (TV, internet, utilities, etc.); me, of the things we *did* (cinema, holidays, dinner, etc.)

The most frustrating thing was that we still had lots in common. We both enjoyed the same type of books, news and TV programmes, especially if they featured any of the well-known people we both admired, from afar. We were still both fascinated by the same geeky, loner types.

I thought everything needed to be perfect for us to love each other. Helen thought we should just love each other, however imperfect things were.

What we could agree on, probably the most important thing, was that we appreciated that the other was working hard to make 'us' work. That, underneath, we were doing everything for the right reasons, even if that was for the things we had in common and not necessarily the love we did or didn't feel for each other.

Slowly, we started to understand we were just very different, raised in very different homes, but that we could work together to surmount some of the differences that caused.

Painful conversations through counselling helped.

At least I was back sleeping in our bed, and at last got to use the giant en-suite bathroom, the reward that ten years pretending to be someone I wasn't had bought.

AGE 39
Perfectionist employee

By the end of the second of my final three years, the business I was finally going to leave a year later was doing well. I was doing the same as I'd always done, working too hard and, of course, still prioritizing being in the office ahead of being at home.

I had once been the boss. I'd had the control I needed, people had done what I asked, I had made all the final decisions. The buck had stopped with me. But, after selling, I signed an incentivized three-year contract to keep running the company, to oversee its growth under the new owners, my bosses. I was their employee. I had little say. The buck stopped with them now.

I wasn't even in control of my own workload, let alone the whole business. There were things happening that I knew nothing about and didn't agree with. I couldn't even make things happen within impossible timeframes anymore!

I struggled to be for others what I'd spent ten years asking other people to be for me. Control over everything is the only way I knew how to achieve anything – that had been taken away from me. No one else knew I struggled of course. I still couldn't share any anxiety I felt. Not that anyone else would understand. My having less control was probably seen as a very positive scenario by most of the employees.

Then, out of the blue, I was called to a last-minute meeting with the CEO and Chairman of the group. Probably not a good sign.

I was sacked.

They said they would send me a letter explaining the reasons.

I just walked straight out of the door. As I had done when I was younger, I needed to get as far away from the scene where something bad had happened as quickly as possible, before my head exploded with the thought that something completely uncontrollable was happening to me. If I could get away I could stop it completely overwhelming me.

I was angry. I had been sacked from my own company! The business I had set up in my bedsit ten years earlier. It wasn't right. It was wrong. It went against everything I believed.

I couldn't sleep, tossing and turning. I couldn't get the injustice of it out of my head. I needed to escape again or do something to regain control over my life.

A few days later, their letter arrived. I didn't tell Helen; instead, I took it to a pub to open on my own. It felt like an important moment. Was I really a rubbish boss? Had I been getting it all wrong all this time? Was I disliked by everyone? Was I not good enough?

The letter explained that my contract was terminated due to me doing 'other things' that meant I wasn't entirely focused on the business, which in turn could have a detrimental effect on its running. These 'other things' included me telling some staff in the pub that I was interested in learning Spanish and horse riding.

Yes, it really said that. It was just an excuse to get me off the wage bill they'd allowed to become inflated and so appease their concerned investors. I was relieved. Fuck 'em. This wasn't about me not being good enough. This was about their business not doing well. I was all right. People didn't think I was a failure. Not everyone, anyway.

And critically for me, it meant no one would ever need to know I was sacked. There were no leftovers to deal with. I could just tell people that I happily negotiated my way out of my contract a year early. That's how I managed to justify it to myself and cope, to park it and move on quickly.

I should have thanked them really. In one two-minute meeting they had cleared my head of the millions of business worries I constantly carried around with me.

All gone.

They say you don't know what you miss until it's gone. Well, I didn't realize how knotted up and stressed I was until they took it all away from me. Ten years of worries gone, in a one-page letter about horse riding.

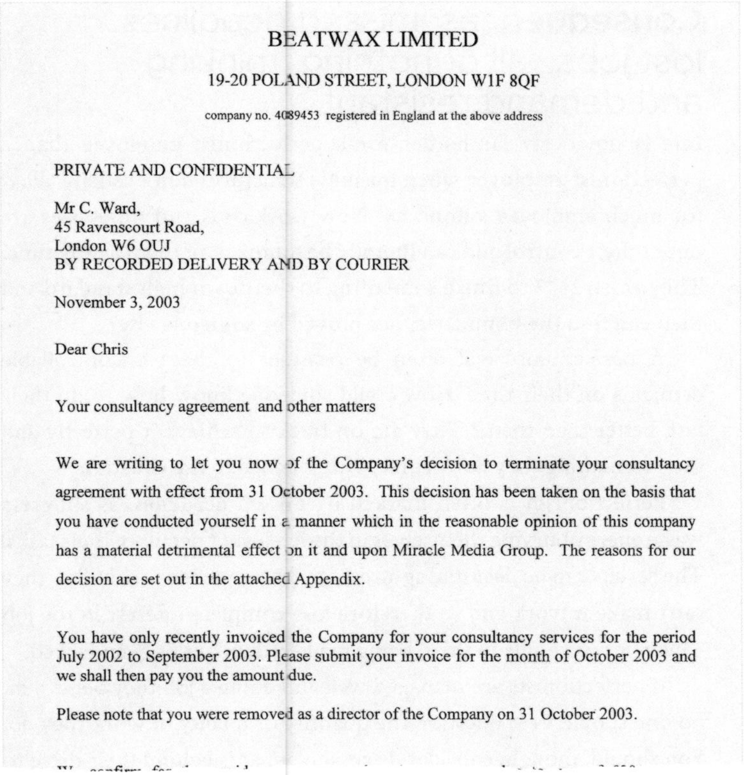

BEATWAX LIMITED

19-20 POLAND STREET, LONDON W1F 8QF

company no. 4089453 registered in England at the above address

PRIVATE AND CONFIDENTIAL

Mr C. Ward,
45 Ravenscourt Road,
London W6 OUJ
BY RECORDED DELIVERY AND BY COURIER

November 3, 2003

Dear Chris

Your consultancy agreement and other matters

We are writing to let you now of the Company's decision to terminate your consultancy agreement with effect from 31 October 2003. This decision has been taken on the basis that you have conducted yourself in a manner which in the reasonable opinion of this company has a material detrimental effect on it and upon Miracle Media Group. The reasons for our decision are set out in the attached Appendix.

You have only recently invoiced the Company for your consultancy services for the period July 2002 to September 2003. Please submit your invoice for the month of October 2003 and we shall then pay you the amount due.

Please note that you were removed as a director of the Company on 31 October 2003.

My termination of employment letter

My head was a clean sheet of paper again. Business was just a game and I'd simply lost a turn. I didn't pass 'Go', though. I went straight to a cycle shop and bought a load of Lycra clothing.

I was already thinking about my next idea.

Consequences: missed deadlines, lost jobs, 'all or nothing' thinking and demand resistant.

Life is obviously far harder for a perfectionist employee than a perfectionist employer when business structures don't usually allow for much employee autonomy. New workloads and timescales are out of their control and can literally be dumped on them at any time. They work 24/7 to finish something to their own high standard and then can find the boundaries are moved by someone else.

A perfectionist will often be resistant to these uncontrollable demands on their time. How could someone know how to do their task better than them? They are on track to achieve it perfectly and then something they don't agree with is added to the equation.

Perfectionism is often marked by missed deadlines, as sufferers waste energy burying themselves in the irrelevant details of their tasks. The results can be devastating stress, or the employee concluding they can't make it work and so therefore lose complete interest in the job – even if this results in them being made redundant or even sacked.

If perfectionists are managed well and doing a job they believe in, no one should ever question the quantity or quality of work they do. You should, though, consider discussing what is behind their drive to provide perfection for you. They could be making a major sacrifice in another part of their life to achieve their best for you.

To have the clearest working relationship with a perfectionist employee, first take time to understand what is behind their obsession to produce the perfect work for you. Then brief them fully, allow them the freedom to produce what you require and, finally, ask them how they would prefer you gave your constructive feedback. Clear guidelines that you both agree with, will help both parties considerably.

:(Part Four :)

Repercussions

AGE 40
Procrastinator

'Is life better before, or after, you reach forty?' I asked a thousand 'suits' at a conference I was speaking at, actually on my own big day.

It was the last thing I did as a CEO of my business, presenting on how we had made Friends Reunited successful, to a cruise ship full of marketing executives.

'After!' shouted one of the delegates. 'But only for the first few hours!'

Right or wrong? I didn't know, but I was determined to make it after, but hopefully for slightly longer than that evening, my fortieth birthday, which I'd naturally chosen to spend on a ship at a marketing conference with a client, and not at home with my wife and children.

Now, a few weeks later, newly sacked, I was free from a job. I was a rat without the pressures of a race he always had to win. Forty and the chance for a new life – it's meant to begin now, isn't it?

What should I do? Take a pit stop and re-enter the same race? NO!

That would be madness. Even I could see that most of our problems at home were caused by me dedicating too much time, thought and effort to work. They say insanity is doing the same thing over and over again and expecting different results. I'm not insane.

So, what if I dedicated myself to something more constructive instead? Could I make my marriage and my relationship with my kids better?

Achieving some success through work didn't reduce my obsession to achieve the impossible; it just meant I needed to look elsewhere now, as that obviously wasn't the right place. Maybe my personal life then …

I was a perfectionist, with my whole life ahead of me and the need to come up with the answer as to how I might be able to make it perfect *before* I even started trying to actually achieve it.

Time to put my thinking hat on …

Symptom: procrastination

Perfectionists procrastinate better, longer and harder than anyone else. It's the one thing they are guaranteed to achieve perfection in.

As their projects need to be perfect, and as perfection is impossible to achieve, they can come up with any excuse to delay making the decision as to whether to commit to one and start yet another long, endless round of workaholism. Any excuse is good enough: 'It's not the right time', 'I haven't got everything I need', I don't feel quite right', even 'This table has got a slightly wobbly leg.' Anything.

Because, once they start, they have to be full-on, 24–7, everything. Everyone else, once again, becomes a distraction to their obsession. With all that ahead, you'd put off starting. You'd want to be 100 per cent convinced you were about to do the right thing before you get anywhere near starting.

Perfectionists find it incredibly frustrating, though. They beat themselves up about being lazy, while they just carry on using all their time not starting a project, but just thinking about whether they'll be able to complete every aspect of it perfectly.

How can a perfectionist stop procrastinating and start something?

Ideally, by believing not everything needs to be perfect! But until then by using artificial deadlines.

I used what other people referred to as 'your kids'. The children needed looking after, dropping off and picking up. In-between times, that was my time to procrastinate, make decisions and make something happen. I had no choice but to finish in time for them.

I could make my decisions and work last all day, trying to make it perfect, but if the kids needed attending to, I could complete it in half the time.

Without being a perfectionist, without procrastination, I can always complete my work in half the time.

AGE 41
Perfectionist sports player

Three hundred and sixty-five long days later, I still hadn't started anything new. I was still staring at the sheet of white paper that lined the inside of my head. I was still not confident enough to give up all my ideas, to commit to just one that I thought I could make perfect. I was still wasting my time, still wasting my life away.

It did mean I had a head free from the stresses that normally overloaded me, so Helen was enjoying the opportunity to be able to relax a little around me.

'We're getting on. Don't spoil it.'

I did need to do something, however – something to maintain a feeling of worthiness. Selling a business brought me a few month's grace but it was time to show that I'm a hardworking, productive, worthy, man again.

What would make my father and children proud of me, what would impress people I hardly knew?

Ride a bike.

Fast.

Yes, exactly like my father, I had to become a dad who disappeared for hours on his bicycle. Deep inside, I had always known that, one day, I was going to have to ride a bike, not *because of* him, but *for* him. Becoming a father wouldn't make me a better person but cycling fast would make me a better son.

On the first rides, I discovered what my dad had discovered during my childhood: a bicycle could take you far away from all the demands of a messy life, full of messy relationships, and back to the real you – sociable, relaxed, open and friendly. I was also healthier and fitter. It felt good. I felt good.

When I sold the business, Helen worried I was on my way home to get under her feet and make her life more of a nightmare. Whereas, with pedals under my feet, I was actually on my way out, making her life more of a dream. Without me in it.

I started out, like almost everyone does, with casual Sunday rides with friends. They expanded the area I lived to include not only city streets but also the sights and smells of country lanes, horses, pubs … and coffee stops! Plenty of coffee stops.

These rides expanded my very small social circle to include more likeminded people. Cycling is a social leveller, with zero class distinction or fashion sense. Conversation was mixed with laughter, about how much cake we could eat now that no calorie was a bad calorie.

Riding side by side, and not sitting face to face, we travelled along in the seating arrangement men need to be able to be honest with each other, discussing our lives, or at least our ideal vision of it. We shared personal secrets and dreams of moving to the countryside and opening the very best cycling café, all without having to look each other in the eye.

Those Sunday rides became a weekly free rehab session in the countryside. A time to live in the moment, escape information and demand overload, mentally relax, contemplate nature but also physically push myself and eat lots of calories.

Perfect.

Success was only about getting home tired and knowing we had got our clothing exactly right. Not too cold, not too hot, not sunburnt and not wet through.

I enjoyed this, far more than I thought I would, and started to join in on some cycle trips abroad, where the feeling lasted not just for a few hours but for a few days, or even a few weeks. Europe was like cycling at home but on steroids – more sun, countryside, cake and coffee. I could eat and drink twice as much and be even further away from my stresses. It was like being on holiday with my geeky mates on bikes from school.

Also, I was lucky. While all the others all had to gain 'brownie points' to get permission from their partners for each trip, I didn't have to ask because Helen loved sport, so she understood why I needed to do this.

Well, that's what I wanted to believe, rather than it being because she was happy to see the back of me, so she could look after our kids without my nonstop interference.

Instead of riding over potholes, I was riding over the Pyrenees, Alps and Dolomites. There was nothing better than working with likeminded cyclists to ride over a mountain range, working as hard as we could, while enjoying the best views in the world. It turned us into friends for life.

I loved this life! It felt like I was actually doing something for myself and not for the approval of others. Unfortunately, though, I didn't start riding to love it. I started riding to gain the approval of others.

So, I moved on to the next stage – doing it for my father. I would prove I really was worth him putting his arm around me and telling me 'Well done!' He would not be able to stop himself showing how much he loved me. He would be that proud!

So, I joined a cycle club and entered a race.

Conversation changed to being about obscure riders and races and what gear ratio I used. I never knew anything about my bike, though; anything mechanical went in my 'nothing' pot.

The experience of cycling changed from feeling green while helping the planet to feeling red with road rage.

Success was now about making my dad proud.

That dream lasted until the end of my first race – an hour around a mile-long circuit on a windy park, in the middle of nowhere. It was a beginners' race ('Cat. 4' as they called us). There were about thirty riders, of whom only about five actually looked like racing cyclists. Like the others, I looked more like my father, with a horribly bright woollen jersey.

The start flag dropped, and eventually one rider broke free. I chased him but couldn't reach him – 'bridge the gap', as the pros call it – but the peloton wasn't catching me either. I was between the leader and everyone else and with only five laps to go. I gave it everything. My dad would be proud of me, I thought.

My first ever race and I was in second place. Four laps, the gaps stayed the same; three, two, one lap to go and I was still fifty metres behind the leader, but more importantly, fifty metres ahead of the group. I gave it everything. Everything. EVERYTHING.

I finished second. In my very first bike race!

While I packed up my bike all I could think about was calling Dad, to tell him everything that had just happened, in exacting and exciting detail, in a way that I knew only he would understand and appreciate. And I knew he'd be proud of it. I'd just come second! Second, did you hear!?

'Dad, I just came second!'

He didn't say, 'Well done!' He just replied matter-of-factly, 'Probably the best riders weren't out today.'

I drove home and tried to explain to Helen how he had reacted but I just couldn't stop the tears rolling slowly down my face. I wasn't going to impress him, whatever I did, whatever I achieved. It was a big lesson I needed to heed.

So, of course I decided to just go back to enjoying cycling with friends, on sunny days in the countryside ... I wish.

No, obviously, instead I thought, 'I'll show him. I'll prove him wrong. I'll do something even more impressive ...'

I would run a marathon, even though I'd never, ever felt any inclination to run twenty-six miles. The furthest I'd ever managed before was three miles in cross-country at school, and that was only the few times when I actually reached the finish line. It was sheer hell.

But, unfortunately, putting myself through 'sheer hell' had never stopped me doing anything before, if it meant I might get to prove something.

Hours upon hours on the bike were exchanged for miles upon miles in trainers. I managed to get an entry into the New York Marathon.

Both Helen and I loved the city, and I thought we could enjoy a weekend away, just the two of us.

A week before the race and another pointless argument about who was right or wrong, about the same pointless things, led to another pointless week of living in silence and me travelling for a weekend away to New York, to run my first marathon, alone.

On landing, I was more depressed than ready to run twenty-six miles, but I didn't let that stop me preparing to run the perfect marathon. Professional runners would have called my preparations meticulous, while normal joggers would have called them insane.

You were allowed to take one plastic bag to the start line, just for the items you might need in the final two hours prior to the start. There were 38,000 entrants, and I had the biggest bag. It contained anything I might need if I were about to compete in an Olympic marathon with a chance of winning it: spare inner soles, hat, gloves, long-sleeve and short-sleeve vests, thick socks, thin socks. It didn't matter what I would need to wear, I had every piece of running kit I owned with me.

I tied and retied my laces about six times in the sixty minutes leading up to the start. Trying to get the optimum tightness – not too tight, not too loose.

I wrote a sign on my vest 'Do It for the Kids', to motivate me to finish it for Molly, Bob and Rose. The more honest 'Do It for Dad' would have looked a bit strange. I got emotional hearing my slogan being shouted from the enthusiastic and friendly thousands of New Yorkers lining the route. It's hard to run when you're welling up, but they did help me get to the finish line.

'Do it for the kids!' 'Do it for the kids!'

I rang Helen as soon as I crossed the line. We might not have been on speaking terms, but there were a few things that justified the overriding of that relationship status. Normally it was to break the news about the death of one of the well-known people we both admired, but I hoped finishing a marathon was a justifiable excuse.

When she answered, just hearing her voice made me unable to speak. I held the phone away from my mouth, while I kept swallowing, blinking and trying to compose myself. I had achieved something beyond what I thought I could, but I had to do it alone. I wanted her to be with me, there, then, that very minute by the bench in Central Park.

I had a wife and three children. But I was alone, surrounded by 38,000 runners meeting, what seemed like, their 38,000 loved ones.

I returned to mine and Helen's favorite cheap hostel. The kids had put an envelope in my bag. I opened it and sat in the tiny bare room, staring at the congratulations card they had made inside until I just fell asleep, knackered.

Eventually, I tried to cheer myself up. It was one of the best experiences I'd ever had. I wanted to do it again, though, obviously, a lot quicker next time.

That time was certainly not fast enough to impress anyone, least of all my father. I obviously hadn't trained hard enough.

Symptom: over-competitive

The pursuit of perfection isn't just about the classroom, workplace or sports field. It can manifest through any activity. Perfectionists can be 'all' about any aspect of their life. In the UK and USA, we see perfectionism manifest itself largely with regard to appearance, work, sport and hobbies, largely because of cultural expectations. Other cultures, and the way children are raised, may prompt perfectionist tendencies in none of the above, but in activities such as cooking, being the perfect host, parenting or community responsibility.

It's not about doing anything better than anyone else. It's about doing it better than they (misguidedly) believe other people expect them to do it.

The following is an extract from 'Triathlons, ultramarathons and ambitious baking: why is modern leisure so competitive?' By **Richard Godwin** in *The Guardian.*

Everything from reading to swimming to cooking can now be tracked or optimised. What is this quest for perfection doing to our free time?

Weekdays are tough. But weekends? Exhausting! Increasingly, our leisure time is not leisure as our parents might have enjoyed it: time away from the productive demands of work for pottering, ambling, collecting, socialising. It is leisure with an imperative, self-imposed or otherwise, to maximise relaxation yield, compete over hobby production and co-opt every activity – exercising, meditating, making Halloween costumes for the kids – into a dynamic of human perfectibility.

Dr Thomas Curran, a clinical psychologist at the University of Bath, sees a correlation between the increased use of metrics and the rise in perfectionism in young people. The culture of metrics has migrated from the business world into our leisure time via education and public services. Schools have become more results-oriented. 'In an attempt to make the important measurable, we have instead made the measurable important,' was how the *Guardian* columnist Simon Jenkins recently summed it up. This has helped to create a generation who see learning as a numbers game, while Instagram, Snapchat and Facebook have done the same with popularity.

This has changed the way we view our time off. In a recent essay, In Praise of Mediocrity, the author Tim Wu shared his hunch that we are now afraid of being bad at things: 'We are intimidated by the expectation ... that we must actually be skilled at what we do in our free time. Our 'hobbies', if that's even the word for them anymore, have become too serious, too demanding, too much an occasion to become anxious about whether you are really the person you claim to be.'

AGE 42
Back to nature

Despite training to run marathons and compete in bike races but without a new substantial working project, I was feeling useless and lazy. I needed to do something while I procrastinated, tick something off my life-long to-do list. I decided on the thing that had been on there since Live Aid: to see how the world's poor have to live and if there was a role I could play to help in some small way. I booked a month-long trip to Africa to help out in an orphanage.

I landed in South Africa on the very day it was named the host for what would turn out to be the highly successful 2010 FIFA World Cup, five years later. But it was to a different, far less commercialised world I travelled then.

The orphanage was home to 500 children, and consisted of nothing more than wooden sheds and a few classrooms. But it was amazing. The kids who appeared to have so little showed me that they actually had so much more than me – a bigger sense of community, more friendship and more love. I simply had more stuff.

The main thing I had that they really needed was a better education. They were fed, clothed and sheltered but, without a relevant education, wouldn't be able to do anything constructive or earn a regular income. Securing them that education was the answer, but I didn't think that working at the orphanage itself would be the best use of my skills to help towards achieving that.

I knew that finding out what that 'best use' might be wasn't going to leave my head until I had found the solution though.

The orphanage was only the start of a trip where I learned a lot about what could make people genuinely happy and contented, what was perhaps behind the perfectionism that was stopping that from happening for me.

I took a book with me that was recommended by a fellow parent.

This was *The Continuum Concept: In Search of Happiness Lost* (1975) by **Jean Liedloff**. The book was about Liedloff's stay with a tribe of South American Indians, who lived almost totally untouched by the modern world. She observed that almost all the inhabitants were at peace with themselves and that the children of the tribe were happy and contented, unlike everyone back at home.

The following is a summary of the premise of her book:

In modern society we have strayed so far away from what humans evolved to be that we can struggle to ever find contentment, however much we search for it, through being workaholics, taking too many drugs, drinking too much alcohol, trying to be famous, struggling with food issues, having many lovers, through spirituality or just by buying more and more stuff.

This is because most of us have missed a critical first few years of life, living totally in the arms of our parents, physically feeling their complete, unconditional love. This is what we are crying out for, as soon as we are born, and what for thousands of years we had – constant physical contact with our mother (or another caregiver) from birth, sleeping in our parents' bed, breastfeeding on demand and being constantly carried, while the adult goes about their normal day. Until we begin crawling on our own.

In contrast, modern childcare often involves a traumatic separation from the mother at birth, due to medical intervention and placement in a unit for new-borns, isolated except for the sound of other crying new-borns. At home, we are left to sleep alone, still isolated in brightly coloured bedrooms, often after crying ourselves to sleep. We are fed to a schedule, with our natural impulses often ignored or pacified with a dummy. We are excluded from normal

continued ...

adult activities, relegated for hours on end to a nursery, playpen or screen, where we are inadequately stimulated by inanimate objects. Caregivers often ignore, discourage, belittle or even punish us when we cry or signal our needs, or, alternatively, respond with excessive concern and anxiety, making us the centre of attention.

We sense and conform to our caregivers' expectations that we are incapable of self-preservation, are innately antisocial, and cannot learn correct behaviour without strict controls, threats and a variety of manipulative parenting techniques.

All this completely goes against natural human evolution, which did not prepare human infants for this kind of experience. We cannot comprehend why our desperate cries for the fulfilment of our innate expectations go unanswered, and we can develop a sense that our natural human desires are somehow wrong.

If, however, our expectations are fulfilled, we will exhibit the natural human state of self-assuredness, wellbeing and joy. We will grow up to have greater self-esteem and become more independent than those whose cries go unanswered

That Liedloff had included being a workaholic on her list of ways we try to overcome this feeling of being unworthy meant that the whole book hit me right in the face, got right to my core. It made complete sense. Alongside other addictions and obsessions, being a workaholic was just another way we try to achieve that feeling of being totally and unconditionally loved. I could now see my workaholism as a troubling trait, even if as yet I hadn't associated it with the bigger issue of OCPD/perfectionism.

Together with my experience in Africa, where I would see the behaviours and actions the book advocated happening around me on a daily basis – elders carrying their younger children or siblings attached to their back or chest – reading The Continuum Concept marked a giant step for me as I started to unlock the real me. I knew this is what I had been chasing for years. Like many children, I was raised by parents who could only follow parenting techniques they were taught by their mothers or the supposed experts of the time.

I rang Helen. I was coming home. I tried to explain about this book I'd just read and asked whether she would move all three kids' mattresses from their bedrooms back into our room. And would she like to move our new-born fourth child, Audrey, from her cot into our bed? But Helen had, as she informed me in words of one syllable, just decorated our bedroom as a nice surprise for my return. She told me she would 'think about it'.

Solution: nurture as nature intended

Without nurturing babies and small children as nature intended, attached or close to their caregivers for as long as possible, we are setting them off, already on the back foot, regarding their own self-confidence and their own innate feeling of being unconditionally loved, to grow up into a world that tells them constantly that what they do and who are they are is not good enough.

We can blame the commercial sector that has built up around telling parents the same thing – they need to buy this, that and the other if they want to be good enough parents.

It's not in their best interests if new parents discover that actually just caring closely for their child is enough. They don't make any money off parents then.

Your child's best interests can be provided for free. As they always have been.

AGE 43
Perfectionist holidaymaker

I loved Africa, in part because I was able to travel on my own again, just me and the smallest possible bag. It involved nothing more demanding than working out how to get from A to B. So here I was a year later doing the trip again, but this time with Helen, Molly, Bob, Rose and toddler Audrey in tow.

'This should be fun,' I said.

Was that a statement of fact or a thinly disguised demand?

Helen thought, or maybe hoped, I might have got travel out of my system with my solo Africa trip. I hadn't. It had only scratched the itch. The itch being the stress of all the demands in my head. Travelling scratched that, gave it a temporary reprieve, gave me some feeling of relaxation and contentment I otherwise never felt in my day-to-day life.

I didn't think that having the kids along this time would make any difference. I still wanted the trip to be as authentic as possible, which to me meant doing it as cheaply as possible and leaving decisions about our destinations to the very last minute, so that I could take on board every review, weather report and recommendation I needed to make sure we were going to have the very best time, every time.

Helen's immediate reaction to any of my last-minute trip suggestions (decisions?) was recoil, evident in every one of her facial features. It was caused by her recalling her worst experiences of this type of 'authentic' family travelling with me. Her knocking on doors of hotels, in the off-season, in quiet, non-touristy towns at 11.00 p.m. and asking if they happened to have a family room available. 'Yes, tonight, please.' My reasoning behind her doing the knocking was that I had done all the driving, though the real reason was my fear of the acute embarrassment I would feel if I was the one who had to stand there looking like an idiot when the hotel receptionist said no.

In response to Helen's recoil, I would also recoil – at her apparent immediate, unthought-through rejection of my fully worked-out perfect holiday plan. We would then share an uncomfortable moment when we would try to avoid an argument. Eventually, after years of not avoiding the argument, we learned that the best solution was for me to make my suggestion, leave her alone to think about it for a few hours, and then try to agree. It worked: there were fewer arguments and more holidays.

The kids believed that 'authentic' (i.e. cheap) holidays only started with flights on 'authentic' (i.e. cheap) airlines and only between the hours of 5–7 a.m. Their first question whenever a family holiday was announced as 'booked' was 'What time do we have to get up?' They didn't think it was possible for families to get seats together, and believed that having a bag to put in the hold was apparently only legal if the holiday was longer than a fortnight. I think they were also unaware that it wasn't illegal to book more than one room in a hotel and therefore possible to have more than four beds for the six of us. 'Have we got our own bed?' was always the first question as we drew up outside.

Getting into that room involved the family becoming military commandos. We quickly mastered the manoeuvre of sneaking a family of six into a room designed (and paid) for four – from the car, past reception and up two flights of stairs – without anyone who worked there putting two and two together. Or, indeed, three and three.

I thought all this was a hardship worth bearing for the amazing, authentic travelling we got to do. Helen was less convinced. Hadn't I dedicated my life to being able to afford *not* to have to do this?

So, what was the greatest innovation that the internet brought to our relationship? That, without exaggeration, saved our marriage? That meant we could immediately eradicate all tension and know there was a room waiting for us before we set off for the day? Expedia.

Expedia.com saved our marriage. It meant I could make my last-minute decisions at the start rather than end, of each day.

With the help of Expedia, Africa was great – the best holiday, *ever.*

Symptom: make last-minute decisions

Family holidays can often be tense occasions for perfectionists. They may have experienced the joy of solo travel. So fighting to stop their 'escape' being ruined by an uncontrollable family with uncontrollable demands can cause stress and arguments at literally every turn.

Perfectionists reach decisions only when they believe they have considered every single piece of relevant information, because nothing they decide can be less than perfect. So, once the decision is made, that's it – it's final. Anyone querying it will only frustrate them; querying it again will often result in an argument.

Perfectionists often make these last-minute holiday decisions unaware that everyone else is annoyed at having to hang on for this moment. But holidays have far too many variables for that perfect decision to come easily. When that's the case, they will wait for any sign – a recommendation they trust, a review they happen to come across, a friend mentioning it in conversation – anything that confirms that they are booking the right holiday, that they are making the perfect decision.

What's more, the frugality of the perfectionist will not be affected by taking their family on what is meant to be an annual enjoyable break for everyone. They will still be 'tight' and have to justify to themselves every pound, dollar or euro their family encourages them to spend.

AGE 44 (I)
Perfectionist partner and parent

Back from family holidays, there was always a slight tension to home life. The kids seemed a little too happy to be home, hiding away in their bedrooms, away from a holiday spent with two parents who were regularly disagreeing with each other's every suggestion.

My life was going around in circles: ideas were whirring round in my head like me on my bike in the velodrome, going fast but never actually getting anywhere. I wasn't achieving much but it meant I was distracted while I tried to work out how I could achieve. I needed to get through this alone; I didn't need anyone else's input.

This was fine when I was working on my own during the day, but when I brought my distraction home, I became the toxic, controlling, demanding, unpleasant, always-right, perfectionist parent and partner. Not that I knew any of that then. In my head, I was a typical stressed-out parent, just trying to keep calm and carry on.

The kids didn't know it either. They knew lots of things weren't right at home but that it was generally their fault. Probably because I told them so.

Home was not a joyful place to be.

It started the moment I came through the door – exactly the same way it started for me when I was a kid, except now I was the stressed one. There'd be endless thoughts swirling round my head, but at some point on my journey home my mind would try to escape the overload by imagining the ideal scenario that would welcome me when I walked through the front door. Helen would have cleared up the house and have grilled some halloumi for dinner, the kids would have put their school stuff away and they'd all be up for watching a movie together. Welcome home, perfectionist dad!

But when I walked through the door, I wasn't welcomed, I was confronted…

Helen was in the shower about to go out, half-eaten dinners were on the kitchen worktop, two of the kids were out playing sport, the other two watching rubbish TV. There was no halloumi left in the fridge and, to top it all, someone had eaten the last piece of chocolate – my bit, the bit I'd saved!

I wish I could have responded differently – to just take a breath, relax, jump on the settee, cuddle the kids and enjoy watching TV with them. I tried everything to not be like my father. My biggest battle in life was between nurture – what my father taught me I should do in these circumstances – and nature – what I believed in my heart I should do.

Nurture beat nature every single time.

I couldn't stop myself reacting exactly like my father. I had to say something. I couldn't let anything go. The following are some of the classic lines I spouted to either the kids or Helen, repetitively, endlessly…

'Can we keep this place tidy, please!'

I don't suffer with OCD, but I liked a certain level of tidiness. I couldn't cope with a complete mess. I didn't help with tidying at home much, though, as I knew it wouldn't stay tidy, so there was no point even trying. It would have driven me crazy to try to keep the home tidy. So, why start, when I could just raise my voice instead?

'Eat all your dinner, please.'

My stupidly high morals meant I would rather have a go at the kids than let them leave any of their uneaten dinner (my dad never let me). Through constant repetition, though, they did finally learn the undisputable fact that 'there are kids starving in the world, you know.'

'That's not what I said.'

I could only ever say exactly what I thought and I couldn't stop myself saying it. Whatever it was, however appropriate, relevant or honest. The truth can hurt but I didn't realize that. I would defend myself vehemently if anyone questioned what I meant. 'I thought I made myself clear.'

'Why don't you do it like this?'

I could show the kids how to do anything better. I was the expert in both finding fault and correcting it. Finding fault with the kids first and then with Helen's parenting of them because Helen always stuck up for the kids. She let them get away with murder. She loved them unconditionally, whoever's chocolate they ate.

'I'm sorry, kids. I'm busy, can we do it later?'

I was busy doing nothing, except mulling over work, or, even worse, mulling over how I was going to best respond in an ongoing argument with Helen. The kids were bored, likewise doing nothing, but I needed my own company somewhere else in the house.

'I'm fine, thanks.'

I didn't share any of my stresses. I needed to solve them alone. I could *only* solve them alone.

'I don't want to hear your gossip.'

I didn't want anyone knowing my private life. If Helen gossiped to me about other people's, it must mean she gossiped about me to others. If anyone did anything once, I thought they would do it every time. If I refused to listen, maybe I could stop her doing that.

'That's exactly what you said!'

I took everything literally and, if I didn't, I pretended that I did. I could show no weakness, especially in an argument.

'You don't love me. If you did, you would/wouldn't ...'

I didn't understand what was and wasn't a sign of love. I knew what I wanted, what I liked and if Helen didn't do that exactly as she knew I liked, it very obviously meant she hadn't really given it (me) much thought. She obviously didn't love me enough. Helen would tell me she loved me but I didn't believe her.

'Do you know where my clean shirt is?'

I liked much of my home life to be to a strict routine that I could rely on. So, once I conveyed what I liked and how I wanted it, I needed it to happen like clockwork around me.

'Are we ever going to have sex again?'

I wanted cuddles and sex, but I couldn't show that I did through actions, emotions and vulnerability. I could only do so by spelling it out. Literally.

The mornings had the potential to be even worse – unless I could escape the house, and get on with all the tasks that filled my head the moment I awoke, without having to interact with any of the family. To them, it appeared I was there, but really my head was already in the office, working and not wanting to be distracted.

Helen rationalized my behaviour to herself by believing I suffered from Asperger's. Surely, that's why I was struggling to connect even with my own family?

But really, I was a misunderstood perfectionist, judging my family in the same way I felt my father judged me as a child. And I believed he thought I was lazy, it felt like he was only happy when I was achieving something. I thought the same about his grandchildren.

It was more important what I thought my father would think about my family, than what I thought about them myself.

I was aware this wasn't good. But I just couldn't stop myself. The consequence: we saw fewer and fewer of the natural, happy smiles our toddlers had worn as they grew up.

Symptom: toxic partner and parent

Controlling. Correcting everyone. Picky. Always distracted. Believe you are always right. Stressed by unpredicted changes in routine and plans. Unfiltered honesty.

Perfectionists will often argue with their partner and cause their children to recoil from them than accept anything less than perfection as normal, loving and unimportant. That's why understanding perfectionism will change lives.

Symptom: distraction

Once a perfectionist is on a mission to complete a task, everyone else, including their own children, becomes an annoyance and a distraction. They can't leave the project where it belongs during their time off – they carry it with them right at the front of their minds, everywhere, until it is completed.

Perfectionists worry. They worry hard and they worry alone. They don't worry about the present; they miss out on that while they worry about the past and the future – the past expectations they haven't lived up to and the expectations of a future they might not fulfil.

So, they try to control their future, by worrying about it! They play every potential eventuality through their mind, as they believe that will put them in the best position to make the right decision if any of them were actually to happen. They brood on it so much, that they can experience the same moods and feelings, as if something bad had actually really happened.

Parents of university-age children always say how fast their youngsters have grown up. For perfectionist parents this time goes by even more quickly because, while their children were experiencing the unique little moments of growing up – the first time they burped, cried, walked, went to school, rode a bike, ate ice cream, touched sand and so on – they might have physically been right there but they were likely to have been distracted. They missed all these things because they missed 'feeling' them. They were thinking or worrying about something else; in their head they were somewhere else.

Children of perfectionists can grow up feeling they are not important to their parents because, despite their parents being right there with them, they are invariably too distracted by something actually not that important to really engage with them.

Understanding: when both parents are perfectionists

Imagine when both parents are perfectionists and are both 'all' about the actual parenting of their children? Both believing with all their heart, theirs is the only way their children should be raised. But their beliefs differ because the way they were raised was different? No compromise.

Imagine both parents not knowing that it is due to OCPD/ perfectionism

When one of the traits a couple of perfectionists have in common, is that they worry about making the same things perfect, it is unfortunately often a story with an unhappy ending. They both believe, with all their heart, that only one of them can be right.

The end starts with the couple communicating through their children, competing with each other, to enforce their (own parents) high standards and ways of doing things.

Lisa Brennan-Jobs is the daughter of Apple founder Steve Jobs and has spoken movingly about the difficulties of being raised by a perfectionist father. The following is an extract from an article in *The Guardian* by Fiona Sturges.

When Lisa Brennan-Jobs, eldest child of the late Steve Jobs, was three years old, her parents went to court over her father's refusal to pay child support. Jobs declared in a deposition that he was sterile. After a DNA test showed they were in fact father and daughter, he agreed to pay her mother $500 a month. A few days later, Apple became a public company and Jobs' net worth shot up to $200m.

Brennan-Jobs doesn't berate or make excuses for her father. As the co-founder of Apple, Jobs enjoyed enormous power in his working life. At home, he exerted power by withholding things: money, conversation, affection. Nowadays his behaviour would be seen as abusive, but, for Brennan-Jobs, it was normal. It was simply what her father did.

He was mostly absent until she was eight, when he began to take Lisa roller-skating. Grateful as she was for his attention, she remained uncomfortable and fearful of irritating him or overstepping the mark. She depicts herself as an outsider whose relationship with her dad was characterised by confusion and shame.

While Jobs could be funny and perceptive, more often he was severe and condescending. He would tell people that Lisa wasn't really his child. He would decide not to pay for things at the last minute, walking out of restaurants without paying the bill, and told his daughter, then nine, that she would never get a penny from him. After years of neglect, he now became mean and controlling. When she became involved in after-hours school projects, he felt aggrieved at her absence. 'If you want to be part of this family, you need to put in the time,' he would say, and then ignore her for days.

Her father has rarely been portrayed as a saint but Small Fry reveals him as a man capable of startling selfishness and cruelty to those closest to him.

AGE 44 (II)
Perfectionist ex-partner and single parent

Just as in my childhood, weekends once again became the best days of the week.

We were in a mock-up of the café from the TV show *Friends*. Just me and the kids. *Friends* was the programme of their childhood. All three girls were growing up loving the endless repeats, and this day out was a good day.

I drove home, dropped them off and headed off – anywhere. I wouldn't see them again until Thursday. It was the worst feeling in the world. I needed to get away from there before my head exploded.

I couldn't exist in what felt like a dishonest relationship, but equally I couldn't exist without the only honest relationships that I lived for.

This second time we split up felt like it was for real and forever. We sold our family home, Helen's dream home. It had been the purchase I thought would solve everything, but the bigger house didn't bring happiness. It just brought bigger problems. We'd been trapped together by the trappings of success.

Helen bought a smaller home about a mile away. I rented a small two-bedroom flat, so when the kids stayed over two of them shared a bunkbed in one room, Bob slept in my bed, Audrey slept in a cot in the bathroom, and I slept on the sofa.

The upside was that I wasn't lost in a big empty flat when they weren't with me. Just a big empty life.

The feeling of loneliness was so embedded in me that it was just part of who I was. I didn't even think of it as anxiety anymore. I was just drifting around, paddleless, depressed. I was still so jealous of people I would see walking down the road not carrying any baggage. It was a visualization of the dream life I wanted. To be able to live without carrying every single bad thought I had ever had around in my head, wherever I went, all day, every day.

I couldn't offload my emotional baggage, though. I saw the same people every day who had no idea how much I was struggling with the entire weight of my own fucked-up world. I managed to keep up the façade. Not many even knew Helen and I had split up, let alone that I wasn't living with my children.

I escaped further and further away on my bike. 'Riding' had become 'training' and purely about achieving something in my life that would prove, despite my failure as a father, I could still be good enough.

I'd caused my marriage to fail, I'd failed my children, I'd failed my parents. Why couldn't I make it work? I should have been able to make it work. My parents showed me how.

I loved my children.

I just lay on the sofa in my empty flat and waited for the time I could see them again.

Whatever had ever gone on between us, Helen had always let our children stay with me half the week. That saved my life. Literally, I think. It stopped the darker and darker thoughts I was having turning completely black.

I had a reason, a purpose to get off the sofa.

I had a reason to live.

Symptoms: stress, anxiety, depression, suicidal thoughts

Perfectionists demand higher standards of themselves than anyone else. They are incredibly self-critical. When they inwardly lose control of living up to those standards or feel they are falling below them, but still try to appear perfect to everyone else, stress, anxiety and depression can quickly follow.

If they fail to hide that truth, and feel they have nowhere to hide or way of redeeming themselves, they need to find any way out of the situation, and quickly, for their own mental wellbeing. In that scenario, suicide can appear to be a very practical way to make it all go away. In professional sport, this same scenario can lead to rule breaking and cheating.

Six-summit sensation

Micky McMahon

When it comes to climbing challenges, they don't come much tougher than Mont Ventoux's La Bicinglette. The task, set by the Club des Cinglés du Mont Ventoux, is to summit the peak six times in the same day — two ascents from each of the three starting points of Bédoin, Malaucène and Sault.

Last month, Chris Ward became the latest and, at 51, one of the oldest of 13 Brits to complete the challenge. Here, the Londoner reflects on repeatedly riding the Giant of Provence.

I did the challenge on a bike I rented at the bottom. The place came highly recommended, but was a risk. I had to change the set-up slightly after two ascents due to knee ache — but it worked brilliantly after that.

I struggled to eat solids after five climbs. It took ages in a warm car at 9pm to get a pizza down, warm up and get going for the last ascent. My wife left the chargers for the Garmin and my iPhone in the hotel. So many things could have gone wrong — I was thankful that was the only thing that did!

There were about 50 Germans doing the three [La Cinglé, half the distance] at the same time. I rode two of the routes in both daylight and darkness, which meant it was never boring.

There was always someone around, or the next meeting with my wife was something to

Ward's six summit finishes

EVENTS TO TRY

My obsession to have something successful in my life led to *Cycling Weekly* reporting on me becoming the oldest Britain to cycle up Mount Ventoux six times in a day

AGE 45
Staying vigilant
Achieving success without perfection (3)

Helen and I started seeing a divorce mediator, someone to help us split up without killing each other or ourselves and so that each of us had just enough money to live on.

The mediator had both our interests at heart. She trod that tightrope like a gold-medal gymnast. Unfortunately, legally she had to advise us to bring in lawyers to one meeting to help with agreeing a financial settlement. I didn't. Obviously, I thought I could do a better job myself.

But the meeting ended with me walking out depressed, unable to cope with what I thought were the unfair demands of Helen's lawyer. Not for more money – she could have it all for all I cared – but for the reduction in time that I would get to spend with our children. Helen's lawyer thought I needed to give up my unpaid charitable dream to help change the world and become a full-time business executive again.

I thought I needed beer.

The children were at Helen's. I could no longer handle being in the flat on my own, and I didn't feel like seeing if anyone was around. I didn't think anyone would want to go out with a morose, estranged husband and father.

So, off I went to the pub on my own, for a pint or five, to escape another bad day. As always, I scanned through any free newspapers while supping. I come across the job pages. I had been working on a new idea but it certainly wasn't bringing in any money. We were still living on the capital I had got from selling the business. I suppose I'd better have a look through the advertised jobs then … print manager for a newspaper, sales director for a publisher, creative communications director for Comic Relief…

Creative communications director at Comic Relief? The creator of the Red Nose Day telethon, Britain's biggest charity fundraiser, which uses the funds to relieve poverty around the world.

Wow, that would be an amazing job!

I hadn't done anything anywhere near what I could claim to be successful since involuntarily leaving my business five years earlier. And all of the work I'd done was still commercial; it certainly hadn't been for charity. The only thing I had to support my claim to be the 'right person for the role' was that, ever since watching Live Aid, I'd known that this was exactly what I had to do, to help put some of the wrongs of the world to rights. I hoped that would be enough to bulk up my 'relevant' CV.

I tore the advert out of the paper and decided to stop at two pints. I had a job application to type.

Seven interviews later, including one with the person I'd admired for such a long time – Richard Curtis, film director and founder of Make Poverty History and Comic Relief – they finally said they would let me know after the festive break.

I don't remember much of that Christmas. It was impossible to think about anything other than the hopeful and hopeless situations that would dictate my future life. A 'happy new year' phone call did finally come, though. I was the new Comic Relief creative communications director, looking after the famous red nose and working on the TV show. Wow!

Everything, work-wise at least, had changed with the turn of a page, in a copy of a free newspaper, in a pub.

I wish I could have turned the page of my personal life just as easily.

I didn't care how much I would be paid or how much I would have to give to Helen. My parents knew what Comic Relief did and, if the kids had to see less of me, at least they would understand and be proud of the reason why.

That was all I needed to live on.

Solution: vigilance

Perfectionists are unnaturally vigilant. They monitor, notice and remember everything. They obsess about consuming every single piece of information they believe might just be valuable in safeguarding themselves against any future unpredicted mishap, that could result in them returning to a feeling of failure. They monitor everything in their lives to try to make sure nothing goes wrong.

There are a lot of books on what makes someone creative. How do some people just come up with great ideas, while others struggle? They inform you a good way to start is to keep a childlike eye on the world, to stay inquisitive and curious about everything, to be vigilant. Perfectionists can be the most creative people when they use vigilance in a positive way and not only to protect against any potential downside.

Vigilance also creates more opportunity for serendipity; coming across something valuable you weren't looking for. Often a spark for a new idea, that in the echo chamber of social media, is being lost forever.

AGE 46 (I)
Important truths remain unspoken

I didn't see Mum and Dad as often I should have, especially since Helen and I had separated. I knew I had failed them, and I didn't need any reminders. When I did occasionally call, it was always Mum that answered and always with the same question, 'You're still alive then?' I didn't get to talk to Dad much, as he'd normally be out on his bike. Mum only called me once in a blue moon. Dad never called.

Mum called.

It was at the end of a good day at Comic Relief. I was in a pub with my oldest mate and best man. We were watching an England football match.

'Something is wrong with your dad. He isn't saying anything.'

That didn't sound too out of the ordinary.

I travelled down to see them, however.

He wasn't saying anything because he'd had a massive stroke while he was riding his bike. His friend saw him fall off and try to remount by sitting on the back wheel instead of the saddle. Dad suggested he was OK, and they rode home. At first, Mum didn't realize anything was amiss, apart from the fact that Dad had stopped talking.

By the following morning, though, he was in a hospital bed. He had had a major stroke, but they also informed us he had Alzheimer's. He still had full use of his body but he had lost a huge amount of his cognitive functions.

We should have noticed something was wrong a long while before. But, in hindsight, Dad had hidden his deterioration well. He'd kept himself to himself, while keeping his conversation to what he knew best – cycling routes and the amount of traffic on them. He had become an expert at nodding and smiling in all the right places. Now he only just about knew where he was and who we were.

This was the man I'd spent my whole life in awe of, slightly scared of and needing to impress. And now he looked like a vulnerable child. I wanted to talk to him about everything. I want to tell him I loved him.

But I couldn't. Obviously, I couldn't. I couldn't start now.

I could have a full-on argument with my wife about the least important thing in our whole lives but I couldn't have a simple conversation with my father about the most important thing – him and me; father and son.

Instead, I just ploughed on with small talk. It was for the best. That particular can of worms was too big to open now and it was also very out of date.

It would be too painful for two men who never displayed any emotions, except for maybe annoyance and frustration, to open up about the most emotional thing. Impossible. Our whole father–son relationship was built on not sharing emotions. We weren't about to start now.

The potential impact of anything we might say to each other was too big a risk. I couldn't go there. However much I may have wanted to. However much he may have wanted to

Consequence: shallow relationships

Perfectionists cannot stop themselves being honest, to the point of being hurtful to other people, but when it comes to saying something that would result in making themselves vulnerable, opening up a conversation about how they really feel, that's almost impossible.

This is obviously why it can be almost impossible for perfectionists to enjoy good, strong, honest relationships. Why a feeling of loneliness can overwhelm them, despite their being surrounded by people who love them.

AGE 46 (II)
Important truths are heard

I was slowly learning to cope with life separated from Helen. We both had just enough money and time with the kids. The darkness I was clouded in had lifted slightly because I was able to contribute something to a cause I believed in. I relaxed slightly. That meant Helen could also relax slightly.

We were able to communicate enough with each other to even consider seeing a counsellor, someone whom a friend had highly recommended. We might have given up on each other but we hadn't given up on providing a family home for our children. We just couldn't – we had both been taught that. And we both loved them too much.

We had a few sessions with him and agreed he was good for us. Was this finally a person who could help us find the answer to how we could be happy together?

During one session he interrupted another sparring match we were having, about something completely unimportant.

'Is it possible you could see one another as children? Listen to what each of you are saying, as if it was coming out of the mouth of the child inside you both? If your children said the things you are saying to each other, would you defend yourself, retaliate or reiterate your own point of view? Or would you find out why they think like that? Why they are angry or upset? Why they might be really trying to get your attention?'

That makes sense. Yes, we can try.

We really tried, and worked hard at it.

Arguments certainly didn't end – children argue, after all. But eventually we actually started to enjoy the things we had in common again. There were still a lot: friends, culture, our children, our history.

Something that simple made such a huge difference. I knew the real me was the child I left behind. And I knew that was who I wanted Helen to see. It's who I wanted everyone to see. The counsellor gave me an opportunity, permission even, to let him be seen, to have a voice again. I wanted Helen to see and hear me as I had been before, when I was a child, free from any care or concern in the world. Free from needing everything to be perfect.

That's the real me. Not this one. I knew that, but Helen didn't – she'd only ever met him occasionally.

We both smiled. Actually smiled, *outwardly*. We could both see these smiles. They felt good.

We laughed at things no one else would understand. Like our children. It felt that, as children, we were made for each other. Problems only arose when we judged each other by our parents' standards, not our own. When those judgements took on competing roles in the upbringing of our parent's grandchildren, that's when the unsolvable problems arose.

Our parents weren't made for each other but perhaps we were.

I hoped so because, despite having said and acted the worst we possibly could towards each other and our children having been witnesses to much of it, I gave up the lease on the two-bedroom flat to move back in with my family.

Everyone was happy … but nervous.

Solution: listening with kindness and curiosity

We are in a world where mindfulness has become a popular way to deal with the stresses of life, while we have been led away from being mindful of other people.

Our world constantly judges whether everything we do is perfect … However as all mental health experts will tell you, the perfection demanded of us is impossible to achieve. That we are, in fact, happiest when we can be ourselves in the company of other people.

Friendful Gatherings were set up to provide the time, for less perfect, more happy people to meet and share friendship, stories and time together. (see Friendfulness booklet)

Alain de Botton is a Swiss-born British philosopher and author whose books mix philosophy and musings on everyday life. This is an extract from his book *The Course of Love.*

The child teaches the adult something else about love: that genuine love should involve a constant attempt to interpret with maximal generosity what might be going on, at any time, beneath the surface of difficult and unappealing behaviour.

The parent has to second guess what the cry, the kick, the grief for the anger is really about. And what marks out this project of interpretation – and makes it so different from what occurs in the average adult relationship – is its charity.

Parents are apt to proceed from the assumption that their children, though they may be troubled or in pain, are fundamentally good. As soon as the particular pain that is jabbing them is correctly identified, they would be restored to native Innocence.

When children cry, we don't accuse them of being mean or self-pitying; we wonder what has upset them. When they bite, we know they must be frightened or momentarily vexed. We are alive to the insidious effects that hunger, a tricky digestive tract or lack of sleep may have on mood.

How kind we would be if we managed to import even a little of this Instinct into adult relationships – if here, too, we could look past the grumpiness and viciousness and recognise the fear, confusion and exhaustion which almost invariably underlie them.

This is what it would mean to gaze upon the human race with love.

AGE 47
Keep it simple
Achieving success without perfection (4)

Graham Norton wearing a red nose for Comic Relief

One of my roles at Comic Relief was to be part of the team creating the new Red Nose, the simple iconic product of my childhood, of my own children's childhood, where the whole £1 purchase price goes to good causes. I had gone from a nobody to somebody involved in something so well known. Ridiculous!

Comic Relief created a new nose for every Red Nose Day, one that would hopefully inspire millions of parents to pay for it and 10 million school children to wear it. I was informed early on that sales of the noses had actually declined over the preceding few years. From a peak of 10 million, the last one had sold only 6 million. It was a serious issue that needed a solution. There was at least £4 million for good causes at stake.

Surely, there must be a way of getting sales and income back up to 10 million but how?

There were plenty of meetings on the issue. There are always plenty of meetings in the charity world – everyone is invited to give their opinion. I thought I might struggle with that.

My head whirled into action, for all of two minutes …

How would a commercial business look at the same problem – declining sales to their large core market of customers? Would they try to attract new customers, when their core product had almost halved in sales? I thought not. Instead, from what I could see, they would look to increase sales from their existing customers by increasing the choice, and then build up again from there.

So, looking at it like that, the solution was simple and obvious.

'Comic Relief should have more than one red nose,' I said. 'We should have three. So the core supporters who buy one might collect all three. They might have more than one child, each child can have a different nose, or more than one nose.'

Finally, after everyone had voiced their opinion again, the decision was made.

Comic Relief would sell three red noses: three characters called 'This One', 'That One' and 'The Other One'.

Ten million noses sold out.

It's one of the simplest ideas I've ever had and certainly the most valuable. Millions more were raised for good causes on the back of an idea that took only moments to think of.

It's probably the idea I'm most proud of from my whole working life.

Solution: keep it simple!

A new idea is a very straightforward concept. It is simply the adding together of two ideas, things, thoughts, that already exist, but haven't been put together before.

Voilà, a new idea!

The best new ideas are the very obvious ones, where our reaction is 'Why didn't I think of that?' They are the ones that succeed, the ones we love the most.

We didn't spend hours upon hours, weeks upon weeks, going back through the entire history of red noses and the sales figures. We didn't have to phone home and apologize for missing dinners. We didn't have to go home still distracted as we struggled to find an answer.

It took two minutes.

There was no perfectionism involved.

AGE 48
Hard feelings

'What are we going to do with you? You're like the football manager Brian Clough. Great ideas but doesn't get on with his team,' said Kevin. Kevin was my boss. Kevin happened to be the CEO of Comic Relief.

I'd just had my second staff '360-degree appraisal' in the last three months. A '360' is when your team feed back to the human resources department what they really think of you, their boss, without any fear of reprisal. Kevin was just summarizing the conclusion, in one depressing sentence. I did secretly like the Clough/football analogy, though. He knew I would. He was a great boss, a much better one than I was.

Working at Comic Relief should have been the best job in the world, and in many ways, it was. I had an amazing time, played my small role in helping raise millions, travelled to Africa to see how the money was used to best effect and worked with some amazingly talented people.

But, in some ways, it wasn't. And the reason for that was probably largely my own fault.

I thought they had appointed me as creative director to be creative. Which is what I did.

They thought they appointed me as creative director to manage *other people being creative.*

Which is what I didn't do.

I'd already seen this second '360' report on my own, on a rainy evening in a café in central London. I'd wanted to see it as soon as it was complete. I needed to know as soon as possible what everyone thought about me, so I could decide if I could still walk into the office tomorrow or whether, as ever, I needed to escape.

I lived in hope that this one would be all right, that people liked me or at least appreciated I put everything into the role and for the right reasons.

Sitting in a little cubicle, surrounded by students emailing home, I read that some of the team I'd worked with for the last year thought I hadn't involved them, that I didn't think they were very good, that I didn't care about them. It was depressing. I did. I honestly did.

But I wasn't just *bad* at showing I cared, I just couldn't do it *at all.* I'd only just worked out how to show my wife of sixteen years that I actually cared about her, and that was only possible by imagining us as children. Showing I cared about real grown men and women certainly wasn't in the offing, at least not yet.

Overall, though, I thought it wasn't too bad. It did seem that most people appreciated I was only working everyone hard so that our creative team could achieve the best for Comic Relief, to help raise the most money for good causes. I believed that was our sole priority, to do the best we could for people that needed it.

I noticed that my best 'reviews' were coming from the people who I thought produced the best work and the worst from the ones I didn't. Praising people for work that wasn't up to my standards also wasn't on the agenda, not yet.

As I said, at least some of this was no doubt my own fault.

After the first '360', Comic Relief provided me with a HR consultant to help me understand that the people on my team were actually human and not just a resource. We had some good conversations, where I was honest about home life and how I struggled. 'You should let people see this vulnerable side of you,' she offered.

But here I was, six months later with Kevin, and, from his point of view, not a lot of my vulnerable side appeared to have been shown in the interim.

After the meeting, I went downstairs to see a fellow director. She seemed to imply that I could solve it just by being nicer. Just like that. We got into an argument as I defended myself. But two minutes later it ended with me, the 'emotionless man', once again displaying the emotions I just couldn't hold in. How could I be so misunderstood?

'You should let people see this vulnerable side of you,' she offered.

I was learning to, trying to. But I couldn't manage it yet.

To me it was obvious I was vulnerable. Vulnerability was shouting loudly in my head, all day, every day. Couldn't anyone else hear it?

Solution: sharing vulnerabilities

Everyone needs to be able to share their vulnerabilities, what they view as their private anxieties and failures, with others; otherwise the stress of hiding them can destroy their life.

The only way perfectionists can do that is if everyone understands what perfectionism/OCPD actually is, as much as they do OCD. We know what OCD is, and we don't make fun or criticize people who suffer with it. We don't pressure them to change. We don't dislike them. We try to understand them.

We don't tell depressed people to just cheer up, but we do continue to tell perfectionists that what they've done is already good enough and that they should be able to complete tasks faster.

Perfectionism is very misunderstood and little supported within HR departments, counselling sessions, marriage guidance, the media or in schools and universities. But imagine if we did understand the damage perfectionism can cause to sufferers' mental health and their relationships with colleagues and everyone they love. They would not need to hide their vulnerability. Their humanity would be welcomed.

Fully understanding OCPD/perfectionism would help us eradicate it and the damage it causes to many sons, brothers, husbands, fathers, daughters, sisters, wives and mothers.

Brené Brown is an American research professor at the University of Houston. She has spent the past two decades studying courage, vulnerability, shame and empathy and is the author of five number-one *New York Times* bestsellers. The following is an extract from T*he Gifts of Imperfection.*

I also see courage in myself when I'm willing to risk being vulnerable and disappointed. For many years, if I really wanted something to happen, an invitation to speak at a special conference, a promotion, a radio interview, I pretended that it didn't matter that much. If a friend or colleague would ask, 'Are you excited about that television interview?' I'd shrug it off and say, 'I'm not sure. It's not that big of a deal.' Of course, in reality, I was praying that it would happen.

It's only in the last few years that I've learned that playing down the exciting stuff doesn't take the pain away when it doesn't happen. It also creates a lot of isolation. Once you've diminished the importance of something, your friends are not likely to call and say, 'I'm sorry that didn't work out. I know you were excited about it.'

Now when someone asks me about the potential opportunity that I'm excited about, I'm more likely to practice courage and say, 'I'm so excited about the possibility. I'm trying to stay realistic, but I really hope it happens.' When things haven't panned out, it's been comforting to be able to call a supportive friend and say, 'Remember that event I told you about? It's not going to happen, and I'm so bummed.'

AGE 49
Loved

The Alzheimer's had continued to steal from Dad more of who he was every single day.

Mum had been doing everything to stop him slowly dying. Alzheimer's is terrible, though more for the carer than for the sufferer. The carer understands what's happening and the final place it's heading to.

Dad had started becoming angry for no reason, believing something had happened when it hadn't, suddenly finding himself in a totally different period of his life and asking for his mother, boiling the kettle with no water in it, disappearing and being brought back home by the police.

I sometimes went home and took Dad out for cycle rides. He didn't know who I was anymore but he'd still get annoyed at me for no apparent reason and still know the route to the local café.

That was my dad.

Dad and I never truly spoke when we were father and son but now we were father and friendly stranger we managed to. Mum also wanted to talk about him, to remember the good times that would keep her going through these bad ones. I learned more about this man who never spoke about himself in just a few conversations than I had ever done in the previous forty years.

This was my dad.

Both his parents were incredibly hardworking. Like Dad, his father was a real man, a proud man. I remember finding him quite gruff and was always slightly nervous of him when I was small. He'd always be showing us what he'd been doing or how we could do it ourselves.

I never thought of my dad as Grandad's son. They were just two men I looked up to. I wondered what my dad thought of his dad? Were they close? Did they ever really talk? Did he ever cuddle him? Or was he nervous of him, too?

I learned that, before Mum, Dad proposed to another girl but while he was abroad on National Service he received a letter from this fiancée telling him it was all over. Not great.

He'd also been made redundant, twice. Redundancy is always tough to deal with. The worry about finding a new job, the stress caused by being at home in each other's way all day, the lack of money and the uncertainty. And this was from a time when redundancy was far less common.

He and Mum had kept all that from us children. It probably explains why Mum was often working her two jobs. I don't know about Dad's self-esteem, but if he was anything like me he would have suffered. He would also have escaped it all on his bike. He wouldn't want anyone to know and wouldn't have been able to share his worries.

If he was anything like me.

It might explain us not knowing when we were small which dad was going to come through the door each evening: the happy one, hungry for dinner, or the moody one, distracted by his worries about providing for his family.

And yes, Mum confirmed, both Dad and she were perfectionists.

These stories and what was going on right in front of my face weren't about the untouchable, superhero dad I always thought he was. They were about a normal man, insecure and vulnerable, but finding it impossible to share that with anyone.

He was exactly like me.

Exactly like many fathers and sons, mothers and daughters.

This was the most important history lesson of my entire life. A lesson not about Henry VIII, Winston Churchill or Emily Pankhurst, but about my father, the person who had influenced my own history, my life, far more than anyone in any textbook.

These were the last rides and conversations we had. His anger turned to aggression towards Mum, as he understood less and less about who she was and where he was. He had to be admitted into a home.

A few weeks later, another call from Mum woke me up. It was 'that' phone call.

'Today,' she said, 'is likely to be the final day.'

I got dressed and was in the car ten minutes later. It was early, so there was little traffic but Dad must have been deteriorating fast, as twenty minutes later my sister Sandra called to see if I was nearly there.

An hour after her call I was in the room with her, Mum and Dad. Even though I'd seen him only a few days earlier, I was shocked. He was flat on his back and skeletal. There was only a very light breathing sound to show he was still with us.

Mum was sitting holding his hand. I asked her if I could be close to him for a moment. I stood over his face and kissed his forehead. I whispered to him that I was there and that everything was OK.

I couldn't actually bring myself to say 'I love you' because that would have been like saying goodbye, and I couldn't say goodbye. I didn't want him to see me admitting defeat.

Within a moment, though, his breathing completely deteriorated, to one desperate gasp every few seconds. Today was the day. The suffering Dad and Mum were going through had to stop. Today needed to be the day.

I asked Mum if she wanted to be alone with Dad – 'Yes, please – and Sandra and I retreated out of the room. I immediately heaved huge gasping sobs as I hugged my sister.

'He waited for you. Dad waited for you to come. His breathing deteriorated right after you arrived and spoke to him.'

It felt like 30 seconds, but it was probably more like three minutes, until Mum came out.

'He's gone.'

What do you do when your husband and father has died?

We went to a garden centre and had lunch. I had scrambled eggs.

We arranged to meet later, for the three of us to go out to a nice place for dinner together and reminisce about the good times.

I had my bicycle in the back of the car. I honestly didn't remember putting it there when I had left the house that morning. I spent the sunny afternoon riding up the hills and down the lanes that Dad had spent many a Sunday enjoying, while I would have been in my bedroom, waiting impatiently for him to come back so we could have lunch.

Riding slowly and just thinking of Dad, about what happened and what my sister had said.

Neither of us could ever say it at any point in our lives. But I knew, with absolute certainty in my heart, he loved me, and he knew I loved him. Just as he always had done. My whole life. Since the day I was born.

Seeing my father show his weakness and, according to my sister manage to wait for me to arrive before he died changed everything I believed about him, our relationship, my childhood, my life.

It could very well have just been a coincidence, but it was so exactly the sort of thing I would do that I believed it.

Like me, he could never say 'I love you', but he could show me. Like he had been showing me since the day I was born.

I just misunderstood the love that lay behind everything he did for me.

I was good enough, I had always been good enough, just like everyone else born on this planet.

In my case I just had a father who was, like his own son, not very good at showing it.

Our love for one another was a victim of our times.

Understanding: unconditional love

Perfectionists don't give out praise unconditionally. They will praise someone only if they measure up to their incredibly high standards. But that is a literal response, not an emotion. Praise has nothing to do with how they feel and love.

Perfectionists can love unconditionally but they struggle to ever display those feelings to the other person.

That misunderstanding, particularly from parent to child, is at the root of so many people's misguided, lifelong obsession with proving they are good enough in order to simply feel the love that they already have.

Many of my childhood beliefs came about, through my misunderstanding of things that were happening around me. The biggest misunderstanding being the belief that my parents didn't love me unconditionally, unless I was good at something.

Understanding: no one's fault

It was clear to me that the events I recalled so well from my childhood, that helped shape me into a perfectionist, were in no way my parents' or anyone else's fault. I do not blame anyone.

They were simply conduits for parenting techniques and societal norms of the time. They were the messengers, not the message.

I've had a great life. My parents did their best, based on their experience, the environment they themselves grew up in and the social norms when they raised me.

Solution: learn about your own parent's childhood

An important part of my journey was learning about my mother's and father's own childhoods, and the drivers behind their own personalities and actions? This process helped me understand them more, and the new, 'perfectly human' period of my life, which included a feeling of unconditional love for others, began with my discovery of such a love for them.

My father's and my last bike ride together, doing something we both loved

Eulogy

My daughter Rose stood nervously next to Dad's coffin and beautifully sang his favourite hymn, 'Amazing Grace'. Like the rest of the congregation, I swallowed hard to hold back the tears.

But, unlike the rest of the congregation, I was the one who had to follow her. I swallowed hard again and stood up – stood up in front of my mum, my family, Dad's sister's family and Dad's old friends, neighbours and fellow cyclists. I began to deliver the eulogy my mother had asked me to write:

'Dad was of a time when men were real men, private people, keeping their emotions to themselves. Dad worked, Dad told us to wash up or wipe up, to set the table and to eat all our dinner if we wanted our pudding. Dad threatened to cook our rabbit for dinner, Dad made toys for us, Dad worked on the car, Dad cycled.

Although I am living in a different age to my dad, I believe we have lived similar lives. When I have reflected over this week, I believe that is due to the lessons Dad taught me and I want to share those now. They have provided the bedrock to both the way myself and Dad have lived our lives.'

Lessons from a 20th-century father to a 21st-century son

1. *Expect nothing more of your children than for them to try their best.*
   Work hard and do your best at everything you try – homework, work, cycling, helping at home. Life doesn't owe you anything. This was Dad leading by example. There were no further expectations placed on us, if we did our best, that was simply enough; nothing more was expected from us.

2 *Anything is possible.*

Dad showed this to me when we went to see the careers officer at school. It wasn't about university; it wasn't about Dad wanting me to be a lawyer, dentist or doctor. It was about Dad supporting me while we told the careers officer I wanted to be a professional sportsman. And to be fair to him, the careers officer went off to investigate and a week later reported back that it wasn't going to happen. It did teach me, though, that Dad thought anything was possible.

3 *Watch the pennies.*

It seemed Dad loved the idea of beating the supermarkets at their own game. We didn't know it was out of necessity. I remember walking back and forth between supermarkets as Dad compared prices and made sure he got the best deal in town for the weekly shop.

4 *Ride a bicycle.*

A bike provides the opportunity to gain the most pleasure there is from life, to enjoy the simplicity that life should be about, to cycle through sunny country lanes, to keep fit, to pass the time with friends, to wear Lycra and to get away from all the stresses and strains (and kids!) for a few hours.

This was dad time.

5 *Eat cake.*

All cyclists have one thing in common, not a love of Lycra or shaved legs but a love of cake, a sweet tooth. Everyone likes cake, cake makes you happy, you can't ever eat enough; but the magic is, if you cycle, you can eat as much as you like. Dad did and so never had an ounce of fat on him.

6 *Put family first.*
Mum and Dad always prioritized us kids, but they put their marriage first. Everyone has stresses and strains in their marriage. It is often harder to stay together than separate. This is no judgement on anyone else; this is a tribute to my mum and dad who so ingrained in us that we stick together, however hard it gets.

7 *It's all right for a father to show his vulnerability.*
Finally, with the onset of Alzheimer's came the last lesson and a side to Dad we hadn't often seen before. He started to show his emotions and feelings, on many levels. Alzheimer's is a horrendous illness, often more for the partner and carers than for the sufferer themselves. But, through it, it was great to see some light, Dad setting the example that it's all right to show your weaknesses. A lesson that, as Helen will verify, I still struggle with.

It's the final one, and it took a lifetime to pass over from father to son.

And it's the one that I'm still working on.

Thank you.

This was a speech about my father but it could have been about me.

It was as close as a perfectionist son can get to telling his perfectionist father that he loved him.

I stood down from the altar and hid myself behind a column.

And I cried like a little boy.

:(Part Five :)

Overcoming perfectionism

AGE 50 (I)
Access the inner circle
Achieving success without perfection (5)

Queen Rania of Jordan launching the 1Goal campaign

A lot of charities were coming together to try to achieve a legacy from the FIFA World Cup in South Africa – education for all children globally. 1Goal, as it was called, would use publicity generated by the support of world-famous footballers to petition governments to increase their financial commitments to education. They needed charity people with experience to engage the business world. That's what I did. Kevin, my boss, agreed to pay me to do it as long as I promised him not to go back and work for him when it finished a year later. He needed a solution for a director who struggled managing staff doing meaningful work, while I needed a solution to wanting to do meaningful work and not have to manage staff…

Five years after I had worked in the orphanage I was going back to Africa, to work on an education campaign.

I discovered that the mobile phone industry was keen to show off its huge collective global reach, in a bid to impress, over the up-and-coming Facebook. It was the perfect match: 1Goal could secure exclusive photos and messages of support from World Cup players and the mobile industry had a global audience they could text them to.

We managed to gain the attention of Queen Rania of Jordan and persuaded her to co-chair the campaign. The queen was young, smart and savvy. She was very active on social media, making a name for herself globally by using her posts to promote causes. She was the perfect person to 'front' the mobile campaign. I secured the interest of the phone companies, while she wooed their bosses. It turned out to be a successful partnership: Queen Rania of Jordan and a kid from suburbia who permed his hair.

One day, we were representing 1Goal in New York, where the music industry was announcing its support for the campaign. Her Majesty was front of stage making a speech about the 1 billion legacy text messages we were sending. I stood hiding at the back of the room, sending just one text to Helen. 'This is crazy'.

It worked: we engaged over a billion people around the world about achieving 'Education for All' and governments were persuaded to commit a further £400 million for global education.

Solution: engage an industry insider

For an idea to be successful you often need the buy-in of the hardest to reach, most senior people. You can spend hours, weeks or even years trying to get these people to engage with you. More often than not, annoying them, more than engaging them with persistent attempts.

It's back to that old adage, it's not how good (or perfect) your proposition is but who you know.

So, get someone on your side who can open the doors to the inner circle you need to access.

I always endeavour to get someone far better than me onboard, someone who knows ten times more or can reach ten times as many people than I can.

I persuade them to be a chairperson or spokesperson, their involvement meaning the most important people take an idea seriously. Sometimes it has been worth giving them a stake in the idea or business.

They open doors at the highest level, make things happen and enable me and my team to take a giant step towards making the projects successful.

AGE 50 (II)

Clear communication

Achieving success without perfection (5)

Learning from the experts *(from top left, clockwise):* F1 champion Lewis Hamilton and Archbishop Desmond Tutu; President Jimmy Carter; Jimmy Wales, founder of Wikipedia; and the film director Richard Curtis

The work I undertook on the legacy of the World Cup led to further work on global campaigns and meant I was very fortunate to meet and work with some of the world's most senior statesmen and women and other leading people. I learned from them how to achieve results, not through the method I had tried for the preceding twenty years – complete workaholism – but just through simple, clear communication.

How they spent their time was more important to them than how they spent their money. So, they achieve their great successes through spending their time the most wisely they can, communicating only efficiently and clearly.

They don't waste their lives, or anyone else's.

Jimmy Carter

I met former American President Jimmy Carter at an event where he was presenting the work of The Elders, a small group of the world's most senior statesmen and women who help achieve peace and stability in countries where these have seldom previously existed through nothing more than conversation.

The Elders believe that in any conflict it is important to listen to everyone, no matter how unpalatable or unpopular they may find them. In return, they will speak difficult truths and tackle any taboo. They don't claim to have all the answers but believe that any individual can make the difference. That has resulted in them using good communication to help with improving the situation regarding climate change, equality, Israel–Palestine, refugees and child marriage.

Desmond Tutu

I was launching a new campaign and I didn't know what to do. Desmond Tutu had just walked in half asleep. I had less than one minute to tell a global icon everything about it, so that he could hopefully impart that to F1's Lewis Hamilton, waiting in the next room and inspire him to help launch it. It felt like I was talking to someone sleepwalking. I told him everything. He just nodded slowly, not saying a word.

But I shouldn't have worried. As soon as we walked into the room he just came alive, repeated everything I had just said, connected immediately with Lewis and had him eating out of the palm of his hand in seconds.

He knew how to 'turn it on' when it was needed.

That's why he's Desmond Tutu, global superstar communicator.

Richard Curtis

I have worked on and off with Richard Curtis for many years. The whole premise behind his cause-related achievements – Comic Relief, Make Poverty History, the UN Global Goals – has been about communicating tough issues in the simplest, most effective and creative way that will engage and prompt support from the maximum amount of people.

He wants as many people who saw and liked his movie Love Actually to engage in the world's major issues. And he knows that, if he's going to achieve that, the content he makes has to be as clear and as engaging as that movie. And it always is.

Jimmy Wales

Jimmy created Wikipedia, responsible for educating not just our children but hundreds of millions of people around the world. But you couldn't meet a more normal guy. I happened to share an Airbnb with him while we were trying to persuade mobile companies to text their customers again – this time on behalf of the United Nations Sustainable Development Goals (SDGs).

I would be working all hours, emailing my way up the ranks of the mobile companies to try to get their support. Jimmy would just get on the phone, call them and back it up with simple two-line emails. 'We need your support. It will help change the world. Liaise with Chris to make it happen.'

Sure, he could call the top people, but I could do the same with the people I needed to convince. I didn't need to exchange days of over-detailed emails; a simple phone call could achieve more. Simple, effective communication in a nutshell.

Solution: clear communication

Clear communication is a struggle for perfectionists for many reasons. They may think that they have made all their points clearly enough, but the trouble is, they can often make at least twice as many points as they need to. They have an unstoppable need to include every single fact that they think may be relevant. This means they are often asked for clarification. Then, irritated at not being understood, they will go on to include even more detail because they can't work out why you didn't 'get it' in the first place. They lose complete sight of the point they were making. And so does everyone else.

Once, after a meeting I held with investors and staff, an investor, who I respect more than any other person I've worked with, said 'Do you realize that they don't always understand the point you are trying to make?' I've never forgotten that comment, and I hope that, by seeing first-hand the results achieved by the best communicators in the world, I've now learned how to ignore the perfectionist in me calling for the inclusion of every single point and instead to communicate my message as clearly and simply as possible.

AGE 51
Perfectionist world

When you do something as a child, are good and enjoy it, and feel motivated to see what you can achieve, everyone tells you 'the more you practise, the better you will become'. But no one tells you that if you compete, many of your opponents will not just be enthusiastic amateurs doing likewise but total obsessives.

It is becoming impossible to compete without being a perfectionist – without devoting yourself to it 24/7, without putting it above all your relationships, without sacrificing everything else.

In cycling, running, swimming, golf, rowing, cricket, there are plenty of examples of the hold perfectionism has over people. They are pursuits that offer the promise of complete control and the perfect environment in which to actually achieve contentment – the perfect performance, rewarded by the perfect result. The culmination of a life's obsession. But it never happens.

Because perfectionism is the excessive drive to be stronger, better, faster, it represents the extreme of self-objectification. Perfectionists change from people into entities who are nothing without the totality of their performance, their successes and their failures.

Perfectionists exist in a world of fear. They don't live in a world of love.

Obviously not all perfectionists are competitive sportspeople. The obsession, suffering and loneliness that can be so visible in professional sport are exactly the same, if less invisible, in the offices and homes of labourers, bosses, shop assistants, lawyers, students, accountants, politicians, factory workers ...

Anywhere you go, anyone you meet could be a perfectionism sufferer.

The following is an extract from the last page of the last chapter of the best-selling business book *Leading* by **Sir Alex Ferguson** and **Sir Michael Moritz:**

There's one final character traits that all great leaders share – from Intel's first three CEOs to Sir Alex Ferguson, manager of Manchester United. It's an attribute that few leaders will readily observe in themselves and few management books will single out. In fact, this impulse is often easier for outsiders to spot and, in the case of Sir Alex was something I gradually gleaned from our conversations that provide the backbone for this book. Great leaders are competing – not with others – but with the idea of perfection itself. It does not matter how many sales records they have broken, how many competitors they have extinguished, or how many breath-taking products they have introduced – a greater, more perfect version of their success always beckons. For them greatness is just never enough.

For the most successful leader in the history of professional sports, the 38 trophies he added to Manchester United's collection where milestones on a journey whose ultimate, and maddingly elusive, destination was the seductive and tantalizing notion of perfection itself.

Perfectionist heroes

Many of us have a fascination with those people that have dedicated their lives to producing something that amazes or astounds us – who have invented innovative products, broken sporting records, created works of art that get to our very soul … They appear to approach what they do in a very different way to how we mere mortals do, with far more dedication but are also surrounded by far more turmoil. We are interested in what drives them to achieve because often, whatever it is, generates news headlines in its own right: perhaps behaviour considered outrageous in their work or in their private life.

They are really inspiring people but very different from everyone else because they are driven, not by the desire to be the best, but to not be a failure. They dedicate 100 per cent of their lives to avoiding that.

Many of the people the world admires as geniuses are in fact perfectionists who have achieved something that thousands or even millions know about and admire. Many leave themselves with too little capacity to maintain healthy relationships, and eventually experience breakdowns. But some accept even that as a genuinely justifiable sacrifice in their pursuit of the perfection that the world will love them for.

Until that is, later in their career or life, when they find their achievements haven't provided the escape from the fear of failure that they thought they would. The acclaim and adulation looked like it might be their salvation, but in the end that illusion evaporates, and what are they left with? A legacy that we all admire, that has often changed the way everyone else following them approaches the same things, that may have even changed the world for the better? … Yes, all that … But that isn't enough for them. As individual human beings they can be left lonely and depressed.

Some are lucky enough to build new relationships but too many continue to suffer or even die without knowing they are genuinely and unconditionally loved, not just by one person but by millions.

Here are a few of the men who have entertained and even enlightened millions of people with their works of genius but who are also known to have struggled with perfectionism:

Robin Williams
Actor and comedian (1951–2014, age 63)

Kurt Cobain
Singer songwriter (1967–1994, age 27)

Anthony Bourdain
Chef, author and travel documentarian (1956–2018, age 61)

Jim Morrison
Singer, songwriter and poet (1943–1971, age 27)

Jimi Hendrix
Guitarist, singer and songwriter (1942–1970, age 27)

Tim Bergling (Avicii)
DJ, remixer and record producer (1989–2018, age 28)

Philip Seymour Hoffman
Actor (1967–2014,age 46)

Chester Bennington
Lead vocalist of Linkin Park (1976–2017, age 41)

Mac Miller (Malcolm McCormick)
Rapper (1992–2018, age 26)

AGE 52
Overcoming perfectionism

Well before my father died, I had come to terms with the fact I wasn't going to impress him through cycling and that possibly I didn't need to anymore. As I had got to know him more and seen his vulnerability for the first time, that lifelong obsession with doing everything just for him had started to fall away.

Unfortunately, what it also highlighted was how much it was ingrained in me – doing everything perfectly had become just who I was. But it wouldn't be 'people' going 'wow' that would prove I'd achieved it; it could only be me deciding whether I believed they should go 'wow'.

I thought they should have gone 'wow' about this: qualifying for the Amateur World Cycling Championships.

Over the previous five years my tempo had risen even further. I'd gone from reading cycling magazines and dreaming to reading professional training plans and having to ride them. Out on shared rides, conversation reduced to almost nothing. I started to wear an earphone while training with youngsters I had little in common with, other than that we could all ride up a hill at the same speed.

As I rode more, my friends rode less. As I pushed on, they would turn off and go home. I was no longer part of a community; I had joined a tribe – of obsessive racing cyclists. If someone couldn't keep up, you left them behind. We were loners in a peloton of likeminded people.

Arch-rivals in bike races will work together for hours over hundreds of miles, just to race each other over the last few metres and seconds before the finish line – that's road racing. There's no collaboration, no compromise, no love lost.

Success was now only about winning.

I twice qualified for the world finals and travelled to Denmark and Australia to compete. I finished in the top forty in the world.

The first time I gave everything, including blood, when a crash in the sprint for the finish resulted in me needing stitches in my arm.

The second time I gave everything up because the obsession to kill myself in the pursuit of proving I was good enough was over.

I messaged Helen afterwards …

> Coffee and cake time – I'm finished with racing. Genuinely. I don't want to do that again. I trained as well as I could. I qualified well. I expected decent things of myself. But sixty minutes in, as we hit the first climb I found myself going backwards through the peloton. Riders of all nationalities were flying past me. I couldn't compete because I don't need to compete anymore.
>
> I spent that first hour racing as one of a group of men totally obsessed about their bicycles, their weight, their entire body composition, and who spend all their money on all three. Men, from all around the world, who, when they discover their best isn't good enough, might well contemplate cheating or struggle with depression.
>
> I know that because I was one of them. I saw my reflection etched in the obsessed, loneliness of my competitors' faces.
>
> I couldn't compete because I don't need to prove anything anymore. The death of my father opened the door to the end of my obsession. The person I've spent thirty years pretending to be is also dying. I think it is only through luck that I haven't too.
>
> I'm really lucky. I exceeded my very low expectations on myself; Dad had never even entered a bike race. So, I didn't suffer the very worst thoughts. But now I've found my answer elsewhere, from its source, the feeling of being unconditionally loved, which we were really all racing each other in order to feel. I know now I'm good enough, I don't need to compete with anyone to prove it.

I was no longer just a number, I was a free man

I never wanted a high-powered job, membership of a private gym, wardrobe full of clothes, expensive holidays or a fast car. I believed all I needed was a result that fairly reflected the obsessional amount of training I put in to trying to achieve these completely meaningless, made up challenges. Small things would have pleased a thin cyclist.

But on reflection, my most enjoyable moments on a bicycle had actually been those I shared with Helen. She was there on Ventoux, on Mont Blanc, numerous other mountains and at the World Championship qualifiers. I thought it was the challenge that I was enjoying but it was really about the excuse I had to share my weaknesses, my vulnerability, the real me, with my wife and best friend.

I don't need to sacrifice everything anymore, sacrifice time with my family or friends for more time alone, with just my bike or my laptop. I'd reached the end of the road and discovered it was all built on a myth. There was nothing there for me that I didn't already have.

I needed to go home. Helen and I were understanding each other far better. The children were no longer hiding in their bedrooms when I came through the door. I was no longer obsessed with proving myself to them, so I no longer needed to compete with the men that still had to achieve that. I enjoyed my coffee and cake. It had been too long.

My phone buzzed. It was an end-of-race text message from Mum. 'I know your dad would have been proud of you. xxx.'

Symptom: regret

I've achieved a lot on a bike. Surely that's good, and I certainly have had many good times. Do I really think that perfectionism is all bad? Being a cyclist, or indeed anyone, who trains hard to chase the win because they enjoy the (literal) journey or the potential rewards is good. Achieving a moment of perfection is great. But I wasn't doing that.

I was obsessed about achieving that win, just to prove I was good enough and to the detriment of all my relationships.

Yes, I've also done well at business, and surely that was in part because, as a perfectionist, I obsessed about working every hour and covering every detail. But, again, I've investigated this thoroughly and discovered that the germ of any success wasn't down to being a workaholic and a control freak. That drives people away. Success comes through simpler, easier, less destructive methods.[1]

Workaholic perfectionism results in lost relationships and wasted days, years even. Time we can never get back. Perfectionism was detrimental to all my relationships, including those with my four children. I was separated from them twice. If it wasn't for the fact that my wife didn't find someone else, someone who actually could show her they cared for her, I'd still be apart from them now. Or maybe not even here at all.

When we were separated I was in a seriously bad way. Much of my life has felt like a lonely existence, both mentally and physically. I have spent moments in hell. I have some serious regrets. Mainly about how I have been around my children. I have argued and told them off for things that simply didn't matter. I was distracted through much of their childhood, and not always by work.

People have told me they've seen me do amazing things with them. But that was me choosing only specific moments to be their perfect dad. Moments, when I was able to compartmentalize working worries to spend a short period of quality time with them. Now I can do that almost automatically: stop myself being distracted, live in the present with them, slow down time. My head is not elsewhere. I can live every single second in focus.

> *'Regret is just perfectionism plus time.'*
> B.J. Nova

1 Outlined throughout the book and in the *'How to achieve success without perfection'* booklet.

The following is an extract from an article in *The Times*, 'Are bad childhoods the reason the sporting elite push so hard?' by **Matt Dickenson**.

What drives the best to push so hard? The psychology of leading British Olympians was part of a fascinating study over four years led by UK Sport with help from University researchers. The aim was to work out the characteristics distinguishing the super-elite from the just very good.

Some findings were to be expected. While the very good athletes focused on winning, the super-elite aspired to something greater, to mastering their sport. Ruthlessness and selfishness were pretty much universal among the super-elite. It reminded me of Chris Boardman once disclosing that when his wife was in labour with their second child, he was checking out a time-trial course.

But perhaps the most striking finding, not predicted, was that all 16 of the super-elite in the study had suffered a critical negative event in their childhood – death of a family member, parental divorce, isolation or other form of crisis during critical years of development. A sense of inadequacy, a core-deep need to prove themselves, instability and often deep unhappiness; it had all been channelled into dominating at sport.

Among many examples, we can cite Steve Redgrave growing up 'feeling stupid' with his dyslexia or a young, confused Mo Farah arriving in England from Somalia heartbroken that his family was torn apart and he was separated from his twin.

All these themes certainly come together in Bradley Wiggins. Born to a violent drinking cycle racer of a father who walked out on his family, Wiggins would find his escape on a bicycle. Teachers told him he was a waster. He set out to prove otherwise.

AGE 53 (I)
Failing and learning
Achieving success without perfection (7)

I'd spent the previous few years splitting my time between my bike and my desk. But then another idea I'd been trying failed. Another idea that I thought was great, another idea I'd spent thousands of hours and hundreds of days on because I thought I could make it perfect.

'It' was a rewards currency, awarded to people for doing good. Just another little idea, then! It started well, it won its own awards, was supported by top names, but I could see the time wasn't right for it – it was too early. One day someone will have success with this idea. Maybe me, but definitely not back then.

Another failure of mine?

I haven't felt able to talk about my business failures before. I have learned to hide them, not even acknowledge them, until I had moved on, started something else and could look back from a position of strength. Fear didn't stop me doing anything but it stopped me telling anyone about it, even my wife, until afterwards, when I knew how it had gone.

I could never do anything that might lead to public embarrassment. If I had any concerns that that could end up being the case, I would hold back, not fully committing to a project, so I could continue to believe that I could probably have achieved it if I had really wanted to, if I had given it everything.

But, in reality, I've learned more from my failures than from anything school taught me.

Everything I know about business *success* I've learned from business *failure.*

The only way it is possible to have success is to reach your limit, learn from it and try again.

It's the same, whether in business, sport or at school: to achieve success you have to risk failure in front of others in order to reach your limit. If you were to succeed on your first attempt, you'd either be a sporting freak, business guru or just very, very lucky.

I've learned, on numerous occasions, that people don't laugh at you if you fail. They are more likely to be inspired that you had been willing to even try in the first place.

Solution: fail and learn

Perfectionism detests practice, detests doing anything badly, detests gradual improvement. This causes perfectionists to measure their beginner's attempts against the finished work of the very best. They compare and compete at everything they are involved in.

Many perfectionist business leaders fail long-term because short-term they can't make the decisions and carry out the actions that might result in any public sign of failure.

They struggle to admit their short-term failures to the extent that whole businesses fail because they can't close a loss-making part or make some of their workforce redundant. It's tough. Reaching your limit is rarely easy. Learning something valuable from it is the reward.

We must all keep failing because that means we are still giving life a go, still trying, still putting ourselves out there, still testing our minds and bodies, still feeling truly alive.

It's taken me a lifetime but I have finally learned that the journey is far more rewarding than any final reward from success. Success comes from beating others to first place, but happiness comes from simply trying something, even if somebody else comes in first place.

Winston Churchill summed it up perfectly: 'Success is stumbling from failure to failure with no loss of enthusiasm.'

AGE 53 (II)

Less perfect, more scale

Achieving success without perfectionism (8)

I was back in China for the first time in twenty-two years, since I had backpacked there a few weeks after Helen and I first met. I was in Shanghai to address the annual board meeting of the owners of the twenty-five biggest mobile phone operators in the world, to present to some of the richest, most powerful people on the planet. A lot had happened in-between time, my attitude to life had transformed beyond recognition.

That last time, I had been alone, going to the post office to see if, by a miracle, there was a letter from Helen, something, I hoped, that would let me know that we were still together, that she was still enthusiastic enough to meet me in Athens on my way home. This time, though, I had our seventeen-year-old son, Bob, with me and I no longer needed any confirmation from Helen that I was good enough for her.

I was working with Richard Curtis again, this time to try and help the United Nations launch their 'Global Goals for Sustainable Development' – seventeen targets that world leaders had signed up to, to end poverty, climate change and gender inequality by 2030. If these goals were going to get anywhere near achieved, then the world needed to know about them. World leaders won't do anything unless what they do makes them more re-electable. They wouldn't spend money on the Global Goals unless they believed their citizens knew about them and would more likely vote for them if they committed budget to achieving them.

I was there to ask the mobile phone owners, for the second time, to commit their businesses to texting all of their customers. Through them we could reach the 1.5 billion citizens who could prompt world leaders to start spending.

I was there because I had learned to think big. What needs to be achieved? OK, what's the biggest thing we can do towards making that happen? Think and act bigger than everyone else, because, up there, there's hardly any competition. Charities ask their local mobile phone company to text out messages all the time, but they say no. No one asks all the mobile phone companies in the world to text all the customers in the world. I did, twice. And both times they said yes.

Making that big request took just fifteen minutes. Outside the conference room I found Bob sitting in a corner, munching on the posh free food. We got the lift down to the street, propped ourselves up next to a street food stall and enjoyed some noodles and Tsingtao beer. This was my new attitude – do the best I can, but without sacrificing life with my family ... If only I'd known this years earlier, when I had walked out of the school gates into the big wide world.

The following months saw many operators commit, until an announcement was made just before Beyoncé took to the stage at a Global Goals concert in Central Park, New York: mobile phone operators had come together to text 1.5 billion people about the campaign. Success without perfectionism!

Solution: think bigger, not perfect

Many people spend their whole career competing with everyone else because that's what we are taught we need to do to become successful. But that's hard, as your potential customers can access all your competitors, via the internet, which means you can only beat them if you are the very best (perfect even) or, more likely, the very cheapest.

But there is this third way: be the biggest – not the biggest business but someone who can provide the biggest ideas. It takes as much work to sell ten products to a small customer as it does to sell a hundred to a bigger one. So, why not try selling an idea that could lead to a million to an even bigger one?

Most of your competitors are not thinking like that.

AGE 54
Good enough partner

Now that I understood how perfectionism had negatively affected my life and relationships it was time to try and make up for much wasted time, to try and repair my relationships. That needed to start with a conversation with Helen …

Chris: My biggest motivation to understand and harness my perfectionism was a quote I came across during my research: 'If you have the misfortune to be in a relationship with such a person, get out.' I didn't want that to be true. I wanted to show that shouldn't be the case. I would like to get your honest thoughts on my traits that I've discovered are in the main due to OCPD/perfectionism and probably the reasons that person felt like that. It would really help with my understanding to know what you think.

Firstly, I obviously always provided you with technical advice when you were probably actually looking for emotional support?

Helen: Agree! I learned this during the course of our marriage but lived in hope you could one day provide emotional support. I had to go elsewhere instead. Often it left me feeling alone in our relationship. There was no point in sharing as I didn't want a lecture from you.

C: I always had to tell the truth because I had to be honest. I couldn't live a lie.

H: Yes, this has proven to be quite harsh to live with, as sometimes the truth can hurt. But at least I have always known where you stood on things. No stone has been left unturned in our relationship. If things were left to me, this wouldn't be the case and where would that have got us? I've never been completely sure what you were going to say – it could be good or bad, with no warning.

C: I hated small talk. I wanted to have the most in-depth, relevant conversation with the person I'm talking to. 'Intense' is what someone called me.

H: Whenever I tried to engage you in small talk, you looked disinterested, distracted and could cut me short. I got used to this, but felt a bit rejected. You are great company out with friends and instigate great, thought-provoking conversations, though, which everyone loves.

C: I struggled to laugh at myself. I took myself too seriously. 'You don't get my jokes' is what you normally said.

H: Yep, unfortunately our humour has been slightly off. Often I have thought to myself, 'Oh, lighten up!'

C: I thought if you were laughing at me, it meant I was obviously stupid. It made me feel ashamed or embarrassed of myself. Which are the feelings I've spent my entire life trying to avoid. Every time it knocked me down.

In the same way that I communicate, I took what people said to me literally. When someone said they would do something, I just naturally expected they would do it.

H: Yes, another sticking point. I would reply to you, then over the course of the next few hours I could change my mind and I expected you to understand and accept it.

C: It is hard to admit, but outwardly I have seemed to care less about other people than you did. I could talk about emotions in a very matter-of-fact way. But underneath, deep down, I was full of uncontrollable emotions, that I was desperately battling to get control over.

H: I didn't get that. Was it that you were afraid to show your true emotions in case it revealed some sort of weakness or vulnerability? This sometimes impacted our conversations when talking about friends or family who were struggling with something because you came across as not really interested and wanted to talk about something else.

C: My commitment had to be all or nothing, So, to cope, I often tried to compartmentalize everything in my mind, which allowed me to sometimes be everything and sometimes be nothing (the nearest I could get to compromise). For example, when we lived separately and I had the kids for part of the week, I did find some positives in that arrangement.

H: Don't get me started! I hated every aspect of that arrangement.

C: However small it was, wherever it was, I needed my own space. I struggled in our messy home. I needed a place I could control to get my head together before interacting with others.

H: Yes, I agree. That was good, you knew what you needed. I have learned how important this has been for you, and I learned not to take your absences or disappearances as a personal rejection, although I did early on in our marriage.

C: I got obsessively interested in doing things, which seemed to inspire people. But I obviously tried to do them to perfection, which means many didn't see the light of day.

H: Living with this has been quite exhausting, when every idea you ever speak about or do is with such enthusiasm, passion and excitement and then you're on to another thing at the drop of a hat.

C: To me, it's not at the drop of a hat. It was only after I've given it much thought and reached the conclusion that I couldn't make it perfect. So, it was then *all-or-nothing* time.

If anything bad happened, I didn't want to talk about it, to stop it existing. I tried not to dwell on things but they certainly affected me in some internal, unhealthy, stressful way.

H: Those emotions you had buried deep inside you. I'm glad to see them now. The real you, I'm happy to get to know you now.

C: I often felt misunderstood, more so by the people closest to me. I felt like most people didn't know the real me.

H: You obviously always tried to protect yourself, proving yourself to your dad and then to everyone in the business and sport world, never revealing your true emotions, in case you came across as weak. But this behaviour continued into your closest relationships, our relationship.

In the past, sometimes I felt it was difficult to love you, as I didn't understand you, didn't see much emotion or empathy, just a driven, determined force of nature.

Of course, I feel very different now, I don't think I could've written this before. I have had to listen, take on board, understand much more about you. The one thing we learnt that stuck is that you were just a little boy who wanted to be loved – that was quite a good picture for me. It meant you weren't the unfeeling and angry person I thought you were, and just that sometimes you got a little puffed up when you didn't feel OK.

C: Thanks! I needed your and the children's love, more than anything else. That's what I've spent our whole life together thinking I couldn't get without earning it. If I achieved, you would all love me.

H: I do want to say, having been on this journey of discovery about perfectionism with you, having read the research, listened to the sufferers and the mental health experts that I do also recognize some of this behaviour in myself. Like you, before you started out on this journey, I thought perfectionism was just about working too long and too hard and mulling over everything for far too long. And that was just the way you were and what has been behind many of our problems, behind our arguments.

But I can see now, that wasn't always the case.

I was raised in a family where being the very best hosts, serving only the freshest food for all our friends, family and neighbours, was the most important thing in life to my father. No one put on a spread like him. At the same time, My mum spent all day, every day, being the perfect mother to me, her youngest child and only daughter.

They raised me on a pedestal that I've never felt I was a good enough for. I'm still trying to live up to those expectations. I need them to be proud of me. I need to do my best for everyone. I need to keep everyone happy.

That's why I've always wanted, needed even, to be in charge of what goes on in our home, to make sure everything happened the way they would have wanted it to happen, the exact way they would have done it themselves.

I think that's meant I have been, as it's called, very 'demand resistant' to much of your input at home. I have been 'all' about these things. I have needed to make them happen perfectly, not my way but my parents' way.

And unfortunately, that wasn't your way either.

I recognize this has been the cause of a fair number of our arguments.

I'm genuinely sorry.

I am so proud of you. You have always been more than good enough for me, and the kids. It's just a real shame it's taken this long for you to understand that.

Helen x

AGE 55
Good enough parent

I followed up my frank conversation with Helen with a note to my children, to explain something of what I had been through and what I had put them through:

Dear Molly, Bob, Rose and Audrey,

When I was a young boy, Grandad never really cuddled me. I thought that was because he didn't love me, unless I was very good or achieved something very good. Without being aware of it, I have dedicated my entire life towards trying to prove I was good enough for him.

If I argued, fought or stopped talking to you, it was because I felt you were doing something that would get in the way of me achieving that, for Grandad.

Making Grandad proud of me has been more important than literally everything else in my whole life.

When people told me to stop working because something was already 'good enough', I knew they couldn't know. They couldn't know if Grandad would have thought it was good enough. Would he have smiled, been happy, proud, want to tell others? Only I could know that, only I could know if something I did was 'good enough' for him.

I was on mission impossible.

Because it was a complete misunderstanding.

Grandad did love me. He always loved me. He was just rubbish at showing it in the way that a young child understands.

Just like I know I am.

I love you, I've always loved you. And I will always love you. I am sorry.

The perfectionism it caused has almost gone. It's time we had some fun.

Dad x

I was no longer on a solitary, lonely mission, focused only on a destination I need to reach before I can start really enjoying the company of others. Life had become about the journey of ups and downs that I could enjoy and share with other people. I no longer wanted to spend my time alone, connected only to the internet. I started to spend my time connected to other people. I felt confident enough to do that, without everything needing to be perfect.

Contentment sweeps over you when you realize that you have always been good enough. Stress leaves you when you realize you can be yourself, and love becomes possible when you don't need to prove anything to anybody and be defined by what you achieve. It felt like no one was judging me, because if they were, I no longer let it worry me.

I still needed to 'reset myself' occasionally, but whereas previously I would have escaped by running or riding away, as hard as I could, I could now share my problems with Helen. It felt a bit strange after having spent our whole marriage keeping them to myself. We had conversations we had never had before. It felt, after twenty-five years, we were only just getting to really know each other.

I could even compromise! Not everything was all or nothing anymore; there were areas in-between that I'd never seen before.

I still wanted to do some things perfectly, but I now understood what the sacrifices were: that I may want to work 24/7, control everything and be distracted. I had turned the obsession over which I had no control into a choice. It was no longer perfectionism. It was about making things perfect but only when I knew I would enjoy the process.

No 'achievement' had ever made me as happy as I was as a kid when all I had was friends and family and all I did was play.

I got to play with our children because they realized that I too was letting them get away with murder, they didn't have to go into hiding behind their firmly shut bedroom doors anymore. In fact, we encouraged them out from behind them, we tried to turn our kitchen into a place where the children could truly be themselves.

Our homes are no longer safe from the pressures of the outside world. Laptops and TV in the lounge and mobile phones in the bedroom are gateways into children's heads and hearts. Helen's and my priority became about helping our children avoid succumbing to the same epidemic. So much of our parenting is about trying to defend our children's wellbeing against all the advertising, social media, schooling and media in their life that too often causes them to believe they are not good enough, that makes them believe they must do and be better than they are.

Solution: a safe retreat

Many parents are losing this inhuman onslaught on our defenceless children by well-paid adults, and don't seem able to stop them believing, with all their heart, that what they do, that who they are, is not enough. Too often parents feel useless, unable to do anything while their children try to prove they are good enough, through their work, appearance and performance, through everything they do, every single day.

If and when they struggle to achieve this impossibility, we see innocent children turn to self-harm, food disorders, alcohol, drugs and obsessions, to numb the loneliness it causes.

Society takes children and makes them feel they are not good enough so they can make money from them. It attacks the self-worth of individuals and their relationships with their families and community.

In our house we have made our kitchen the least judgemental place in our children's lives, somewhere they can relax and not be judged, by us or anyone else. There are rules, yes, but no judgement, no pressure and no mobile phones. It's so safe, we even ignore their normal teenage rudeness here, and tolerate their wearing headphones and lack of verbal interaction.

But it's not about what we say. (Say nothing and it soon stops – they're not listening anyway.) It's about what we *do* – chat, cuddle, clean clothes, share meals, share problems, offer a shoulder or just give them a few pounds, just enough, so they can do simple things together with their friends and their siblings, a coffee, a takeaway or a trip to the cinema. Things that take them off-line and outside.

The kitchen is the kids' 'retreat'. It provides a safe base for their life. We no longer raise our voices here like we used to. Instead, we work hard on knowing what all embarrassing parents should know about youth TV, cinema and music. It's somewhere our children can laugh with each other and at us.

It's a stop-off for them, where we just do what we can to help them enjoy the journeys they are on.

Like every couple, Helen and I still have stresses and strains, but now we understand what is behind them. That makes us more tolerant and understanding of each other. That makes Helen more tolerant and understanding of me.

AGE 56
Good enough life

Back at home, I learned that the Friends Reunited website, which I had helped become successful and whose owners had gone on to sell for £170 million, was to close down. Working on it was, without a doubt, a good time, but what I hadn't reflected on before, despite it being a significant moment in my life, was that I was offered a shareholding by the owners, large enough to have made me £millions when the site was sold.

I made a decision that meant I said no to that offer.

I think it was the best – wrong – decision I ever made.

Part of that reflection is based on my perfectionist self believing I hadn't done anything like enough work to 'earn' that amount of money. I would have been embarrassed to claim it as a sign of a successful life, especially to my father.

But it was only after that decision, when Helen and I were close to divorce, and I needed to earn some money, that I saw the advertisement for the role at Comic Relief in the newspaper. Getting that job led to the most fulfilling and valuable ten years of work I have ever done.

Helen, the family and I might well not still be together, either. I did well enough financially, when I sold my own business, to buy a big house, but it didn't work as our 'home' – it's no coincidence that when we were we reunited it was in a house and home where I could shout 'Dinner's ready, kids' from the kitchen and everyone could hear me. Even if they did still ignore me.

We had been trapped by the trappings of success. More money meant those trappings might well have trapped us permanently.

Even though I had 'missed out' on a huge amount of money, I really haven't given it much thought. The money could well have meant the end of the real me, which would have been buried too deeply while I lived a life distracted by the trappings that came with it. A life potentially lived with the feeling of loneliness and unhappiness. The one I am now free to leave behind.

Free in fact to earn less and do more, like cycling around the world, for as little cost as possible – by bike-packing. It's like back-packing, but on a bicycle. It's travelling slowly with friends or family, to new places, meeting new people, tasting new food, experiencing new cultures. It's taking me back to the most fun and enjoyable aspects of those early days of cycling, to those early days of my life even.

I ride my bike to enjoy the journey with friends and family, not to focus on achieving anything by the time it ends.

It's a bit like a metaphor for my whole life now.

For me, it's been a long journey – from lifelong perfectionist to … well, someone, for example, who's happy to accept this book about perfectionism isn't perfect, but that it's good enough. I have learned to harness my OCPD/perfectionism. I rarely hear the demanding voice in my head anymore, but when I do, I am able to quieten it. I don't need to prove anything anymore.

That's *good enough* for me. It should be good enough for anyone.

Learning: time matters more than money

Money does not bring happiness. Loving relationships and time spent doing something you believe in with people you care about, are worth far more than anything you can ever spend money on. I learned that lesson late, a lesson that can save millions, not of pounds or dollars, but of wasted hours, obsessing about achieving something that doesn't exist.

How you spend your time is more important than how you spend your money. Money can't buy happiness but time can. You can always get money back, but not time.

Earn less. Do more!

Above: with my friend Steve, in Brisbane,
after we'd bike-packed across Australia.
Below: My new Tibetan Mastiff friends
I met cycling from China to Mount Everest

AGE 57

Good enough world

Media headlines about the epidemic of perfectionism

So here we are, right up to date, with media headlines appearing everywhere about the epidemic of perfectionism. The truth will always come out in the end.

We all start out as equally imperfect (and vulnerable) children but we have created a world where constant school testing, parental expectations, and the pressures of social media and advertising, all added on top of the stresses and strains that already cause relationship problems in many families, mean that, by the time we say farewell to our childhood, many of us believe we are in some way just no longer good enough.

We now know it develops, unchecked, into an unseen adult obsession that perfectionists just learn to hide from the world.

We have an epidemic of our very own making that turns innocent children into obsessed adults.

Everyone needs to understand perfectionism so we can bring an end to the damage it is doing to our mental health. We need to collectively reject these messages that make us compare ourselves and judge each other and debunk the mythically happy life of perfectionism, falsely presented by too many successful people. Success doesn't make anyone happy. Only understanding why we thought it would can.

We now spend too much of our time avoiding each other behind screens, when we are at our happiest with good face-to-face relationships with other people.

The world will be far more harmonious when everyone understands what perfectionism really is and understands that we can all be less perfect, more happy.

Solution: friendful gatherings

We have created the idea of Friendful Gatherings for anyone to host for family, friends, fellow students or work colleagues, at home, on holiday or on a retreat. Anywhere with anyone.

Friendful Gatherings were set up to provide the time, for less perfect, more happy people to meet and share friendship, stories and time together.

When the world is telling us we are not good enough for each other, Being Friendful to others is the way to show that we are.

To host or attend a Friendfulness Gathering, check out friendfulness.com or email helen@bluedotworld.com

'If human beings were perfect, stories wouldn't exist because our imperfections create the stories we tell.'

CHIMAMANDA NGOZI ADICHIE